THE ECLECTIC ELECTRIC *Skillet* COOKBOOK

NATIONAL PRESTO INDUSTRIES, INC.
EAU CLAIRE, WISCONSIN 54703

ISBN 0-9654108-4-6
© 2006, 2009 National Presto Industries, Inc.
Part No. 59-439E

Contents

CHAPTER ONE

Introduction

Today's busy cooks genuinely understand the many advantages of cooking with an electric skillet. Its ample contours will hold just about anything, and the touch-of-the-dial heat control produces ideal conditions for techniques as diverse as roasting, steaming, sautéing, and baking. In addition, the skillet's nonstick surface reduces the need for cooking fats as well as making cleanup effortless. And certainly not the least of its assets are energy savings and portability.

In developing the recipes for this book, much thought was given to those circumstances and occasions when the electric skillet's multiple talents would most come in handy. The list began with the obvious: hot hors d'oeuvres for parties, one-pan meals for casual get-togethers, and breakfasts to cook and serve tableside. Then it seemed appropriate to focus on all those times when the skillet could be used instead of the oven on hot summer days or when making several dishes at once for a big holiday dinner. The results were a wide assortment of spectacular dishes like creamy dips, hearty roasts, perfect pitas, delightful frittatas, succulent breads, and mouth-watering desserts.

Yet, there was still more that the skillet could offer! The even, dependable heat of an electric skillet ensured sauce-making success. Recipes with both delicate and robust sauces were natural additions, as were otherwise tricky candies and preserves. The skillet's speed and versatility made quick work of sandwiches, snacks, chili, and stews.

The wide variety of cooking techniques available from the skillet also became a great source of inspiration for cooking vegetables. Broccoli, cauliflower, zucchini, and green beans never tasted so good—whether steamed, sautéed, or simmered in a sauce. It seemed as if vegetables alone would ensure everyday skillet use!

With the list complete, over 200 delectable recipes were developed and tested in an 11-inch electric skillet…and sampled with great pleasure!

However, one size doesn't fit all when developing recipes for a skillet. A 12-inch skillet can typically be used without adjustment. To adjust yields to suit your skillet's size or your family's needs, ingredient quantities can, oftentimes, simply be doubled or cut in half. When increasing or decreasing recipe yields—watch the timing—as small quantities will cook faster and larger amounts will take longer, and may need a bit more liquid. Some experimentation will be required.

Basics

History and Performance

The electric skillet was among the many time-saving appliances innovated in the 1950s. Early skillets were simply aluminum pans with an attached electric cord. Although they captured

consumer interest, they still cooked "hot and fast" and presented a cleaning challenge. Then in 1956, Presto introduced a new industry standard with the invention of the Control Master® removable heat control. This control enabled the use of varying heat settings as well as providing complete immersability when the heat control was detached. Technological advances paved the way for the skillet's nonstick surface, which improved significantly as the decades passed.

The popularity of the multi-talented electric skillet continues to broaden. Today's lightweight electric skillets are available in various sizes. The body serves the functions of a skillet, and with the domed lid in place, it can also transform into a baker, steamer, or Dutch oven. Although the nonstick cooking surface is appreciably sturdier than in earlier skillets, it is still wise to use wooden or plastic utensils.

Fundamental to the skillet's performance is the heat control unit. Heat settings range from Warm to 400°. This thermostat-controlled heating process is quite similar to that of a conventional oven. With the control set at 350°, for example, the skillet will heat continuously until that temperature is reached; then it will cycle on and off to maintain the temperature. Speed and efficiency will vary according to the amount of electric current coming to the home, the number of appliances that share the same circuit, and the amount of electricity being used in the area at any given time.

Cooking with an Electric Skillet

Basic procedures for cooking in an electric skillet are outlined below. They are quite similar to those of conventional cooking. In general, the efficiency of the electric skillet means that much cooking is done at lower temperatures and for shorter amounts of time.

Cooking Rack/Steamer Basket: Some recipes in this cookbook will call for a rack to be used in conjuction with the skillet. For steaming vegetables, an inexpensive steamer basket is the best accessory. For other foods, any rack that is at least one-half inch high will work—such as a small cake rack, wok-style steaming rack, or pressure cooker rack. They will likely be available at kitchen, discount, and hardware stores. If necessary, raise the rack above the liquid by placing crumpled aluminum foil or canning jar metal rings under it. A rack can also be improvised by turning a disposable pie pan upside down and punching 10 to 12 holes in the bottom. Whatever type of rack is used, be sure that it doesn't have sharp edges that will scratch the skillet's nonstick surface.

Melting Butter: Because butter will burn at high settings, always use the Warm setting to melt butter for sautéing, sauces, and other uses that require the lowest setting.

Pan-Frying and Sautéing: As a general rule, vegetables are sautéed at 225° and meats are browned at 350°. The skillet is often preheated so that when oil and food are added, it is hot enough to evenly brown and seal in juices for best flavor. Butter should always be preheated at Warm, even if the food will be cooked at a higher setting. When cooking bacon, do not preheat the skillet in an effort to reduce spattering and shrinking.

Simmering: Simmering is cooking at a heat level slightly below the boiling point. When foods are simmering properly, small bubbles appear, but do not break the surface of the liquid being cooked. In all electric skillets, foods will heat to simmering at some point between the Warm setting and 200°. The precise point will differ according to the type of food being cooked and the environment, such as altitude and electricity level. Heat the skillet at 400° until the food boils; then reduce the heat to the simmer level by turning the heat control down until the pilot light goes out. To simmer without boiling, start at Warm and increase the heat until the simmer point is reached.

Steaming: Generally, foods that require steaming are placed directly on a rack over—but not in—simmering liquid. The skillet's domed lid and controlled heat make it an extremely efficient steamer. Foods cook quickly, retain delicate flavors, and remain perfectly moist. Steaming is often associated with vegetables and fish, but it's also a wonderful technique for many other marvelous dishes. When foods are placed directly on a rack and cooked over well-seasoned broth, wine, or sauce, they become infused with flavor. Steamed puddings, cakes, and breads, by contrast, are steamed in containers placed on a rack over water to maintain their delicate flavor and moist centers.

Stir-Frying: Stir-frying is fast cooking in a small amount of oil at high heat. Foods are cut into small pieces and stirred continuously to cook thoroughly in the shortest amount of time. Meats and poultry are often marinated prior to stir-frying to ensure tenderness and uniform seasoning. Vegetables are almost always added to the pan sequentially, starting with the firmest and leaving the most delicate for last, so that all are cooked perfectly to crisp-tenderness. Once the primary ingredients have been stir-fried, they are usually combined and briefly heated in a sauce. One convenience of stir-fry recipes is that all preparations, including cutting up the food and mixing the sauce, can be done in advance, leaving only a few minutes of cooking to be done just before serving. For best results, be sure that the cooking oil is hot before adding the food and be careful not to overcook. This method is ideal for Asian favorites and fresh vegetable combinations.

Pot Roasting or Braising: There's plenty of room in an electric skillet to cook large pieces of meat, and the domed lid allows air to circulate for even doneness. However, some liquid must be added to the skillet to prevent the meat drippings from burning and smoking. The small amount of moisture required could be broth, wine, or sauce that will wonderfully season the meat as it cooks. The other "must" for successful cooking is that large pieces of meat or poultry need to be raised off the bottom of the skillet to prevent them from burning. Food needs to be raised slightly—just high enough to keep it from touching the bottom. This can be achieved by placing the meat on a rack, on several skewers laid across the bottom of the skillet, on several pieces of crumpled aluminum foil, or on canning jar metal rings.

Baking: Surprisingly, breads, pizzas, pastries, cakes, and cookies can be easily baked in an electric skillet. Bake breads and cakes in baking pans placed directly in the skillet. They will get golden brown on the bottom, but not on top. So don't judge doneness by the color of the top; follow the doneness test given in the recipe. Many of the recipes include glazes, toppings, or frostings. The skillet's even heat and domed lid create ideal rising conditions for yeast bread dough. Set the bowl or pan of dough on a rack in the skillet and cover with the lid. Heat the skillet at Warm for one minute; then turn to Off. Let the dough stand, covered, until doubled, or as directed in the recipe.

Reheating: Set the electric skillet at Warm to reheat foods evenly. Use the lid for foods that need to stay moist; remove the lid for foods that should be crisp.

Breakfast

Good mornings start with the comforting aroma of breakfast cooking. Though the electric skillet has always been an easy choice for breakfast, this inspiring collection of recipes brilliantly extends well beyond the basics.

Enjoy a tranquil weekend morning relaxing on the patio with *Silky Apricot Crêpes* and *Honeyed Oranges and Grapefruit*. For a weekend with friends or family, greet your guests with a fabulous breakfast of *Double Cheese Vegetable Frittata* and *Almond Cream Cheese Coffee Cake*. Start any brunch with delightful steamed breads, *Poppy Seed Pan Rolls*, and *Cinnamon Spice Apple Butter*.

Because it's not always easy to "rise and shine," try *Mexican Breakfast Wraps* and *Vanilla Cream French Toast with Almond Syrup* to perk up your family's sleepy eyes. *Farm-Style Hash Browns and Eggs* will satisfy the heartiest of appetites.

Whatever the reason, let the warm, soothing touch of a fresh-cooked breakfast brighten everyone's day.

Double Cheese Vegetable Frittata

8	eggs, beaten	1	cup small broccoli florets
¾	cup small curd cottage cheese	½	cup chopped red pepper
2	tablespoons honey Dijon mustard	½	cup chopped fresh mushrooms
½	teaspoon salt	¼	cup sliced green onions
¼	teaspoon pepper	¾	cup shredded Muenster cheese
3	tablespoons butter		

Whisk eggs, cottage cheese, mustard, salt, and pepper in medium bowl. Reserve.

Heat butter in skillet at Warm until melted. Add broccoli, pepper, mushrooms, and onions; cook at 250° until vegetables are crisp-tender, about 2 to 3 minutes. Stir egg mixture into vegetables; cook, covered, until eggs are set, 12 to 15 minutes. Sprinkle cheese over egg mixture; cook, covered until cheese is melted, about 1 minute. Cut into squares with plastic or wooden utensil.

6 servings

Canadian Bacon and Egg Breakfast Sandwiches

⅓	cup mayonnaise	8	ounces sliced Canadian bacon or ham
1	teaspoon lemon juice	1	tablespoon butter or margarine
1	teaspoon Dijon-style mustard	4	eggs
½	teaspoon sugar	½	cup shredded Swiss cheese
2	English muffins, split		Paprika
	Butter or margarine, softened		

Mix mayonnaise, lemon juice, mustard, and sugar in small bowl. Reserve.

Spread cut sides of muffins lightly with softened butter. Heat skillet at 275°. Place Canadian bacon and muffins, cut sides down, in skillet; cook until muffins are golden and Canadian bacon is hot. Remove from skillet; place Canadian bacon slices on muffins; cover loosely with aluminum foil. Heat 1 tablespoon butter in skillet at Warm until melted. Fry eggs at 250° to desired degree of doneness. Sprinkle eggs with cheese; cook, covered, until cheese is melted, about 1 minute. Place eggs on Canadian bacon; sprinkle with paprika. Serve with reserved sauce.

4 servings

Steak 'n' Cheese Scrambled Eggs

¼ cup Worcestershire sauce
3 tablespoons spicy brown mustard
4 3-ounce beef sandwich steaks
2 tablespoons butter or margarine, divided

1 3-ounce package cream cheese, cubed
8 eggs
¼ cup chopped green onions
Salt and pepper

Mix Worcestershire and mustard in small bowl; brush generously on both sides of steaks. Let stand 5 minutes. Heat 1 tablespoon butter in skillet at Warm until melted. Add steaks; cook, covered, at 300° until browned, about 2 minutes on each side. Remove steaks; keep warm.

Add remaining 1 tablespoon butter and cream cheese to skillet; cook at 200° until cheese is melted. Beat eggs until foamy in medium bowl; stir in onions. Add egg mixture to skillet; cook until eggs are set, 1 to 2 minutes, stirring occasionally. Season to taste with salt and pepper. Serve with steaks.

4 servings

Mexican Breakfast Wraps

6 slices bacon
¼ cup chopped green onions
6 eggs, beaten
1 4-ounce can diced green chiles, drained

¾ cup shredded Monterey Jack cheese or jalapeño jack cheese
4 flour tortillas (8-inch diameter)
Salsa
Sour Cream

Cook bacon in skillet at 300° until crisp. Remove bacon and crumble when cooled. Pour off excess drippings; reserving 1 tablespoon in skillet. Add green onions; cook at 250° until tender, about 1 minute. Stir in eggs, bacon, and chiles. Cook until eggs are set, stirring occasionally. Sprinkle cheese over egg mixture; cook, covered, until cheese is melted, about 1 minute. Divide egg mixture evenly between 4 tortillas. Roll up and serve with salsa and sour cream.

4 servings

Herbed Omelet Parmesan

	Hot Italian Sausage Antipasto (see recipe below)	¼	teaspoon salt
	Butter or margarine, softened	⅛	teaspoon dried tarragon leaves
6	egg whites	⅛	teaspoon white pepper
⅛	teaspoon cream of tartar	2	tablespoons grated Parmesan cheese, divided
6	egg yolks		Minced parsley
½	teaspoon dried basil leaves		

Make Hot Italian Sausage Antipasto; remove from skillet and reserve. Clean skillet.

Cut double thickness of aluminum foil 20 inches long; place in skillet, allowing edges of foil to extend up sides of skillet. Butter foil generously.

Beat egg whites and cream of tartar in large bowl until stiff peaks form. Beat egg yolks, basil, salt, tarragon, and pepper in large bowl until thick and lemon colored, about 5 minutes. Stir about a fourth of the egg whites into yolk mixture; fold yolk mixture into remaining whites. Fold in 1½ tablespoons cheese.

Heat skillet at 250°. Pour egg mixture into skillet; cook, covered, 30 minutes, or until omelet appears dry on top and springs back when lightly touched. Loosen edges of omelet with plastic or wooden spatula; lift from skillet, using foil, and invert on serving platter. Sprinkle with remaining ½ tablespoon cheese and parsley; keep warm. Return reserved antipasto mixture to skillet; cook, covered, at 300° until heated, 3 to 4 minutes. Serve Hot Italian Sausage Antipasto with omelet.

4 servings

Hot Italian Sausage Antipasto

1	pound mild or hot Italian sausage, cut into 2-inch pieces	½	cup sliced pitted black olives
2	cups coarsely chopped tomatoes	1	clove garlic, minced
1½	cups sliced mushrooms	2	tablespoons lemon juice
1	medium zucchini, cut into ½-inch pieces	1	teaspoon dried basil leaves
1	9-ounce package frozen artichoke hearts	1	teaspoon minced parsley
		¼	teaspoon dried oregano leaves
			Salt and pepper

Cook sausage in skillet at 300° until browned and no longer pink in the center, 8 to 10 minutes. Pour excess drippings from skillet. Stir in remaining ingredients, except salt and pepper; cook, covered, until vegetables are tender, 8 to 10 minutes, stirring occasionally. Season to taste with salt and pepper.

4 servings

Savory Homemade Sausage Patties

1	pound ground pork	¼	teaspoon dried rosemary leaves
½	teaspoon salt	¼	teaspoon fennel seeds, crushed
½	teaspoon dried sage leaves	¼	teaspoon pepper
¼	teaspoon dried marjoram leaves	⅛	teaspoon dried thyme leaves

Mix all ingredients until well blended in medium bowl. Form mixture into 8 patties. Heat skillet at 325°. Cook sausage patties until brown and no longer pink in the center, about 5 minutes on each side.

4 servings

Eggs Scrambled with Tortillas

3	tablespoons butter or margarine	½	cup shredded Monterey Jack cheese
4	corn tortillas, cut into ½-inch strips	1	4-ounce can chopped green chiles, drained
¼	cup chopped green onions		Salt and pepper
6	eggs, beaten		
3	tablespoons milk		

Heat butter in skillet at Warm until melted. Add tortillas; cook at 300° until crisp, about 30 seconds. Remove tortillas and drain on paper toweling. Add onions; cook at 225° for 1 minute. Stir in eggs, milk, cheese, chiles, and tortillas; cook until eggs are set, stirring occasionally. Season eggs to taste with salt and pepper.

4 servings

Farm-Style Hash Browns and Eggs

1	pound bacon	8	eggs, beaten
1	cup sliced mushrooms		Salt and pepper
½	cup chopped green pepper	1	cup shredded cheddar cheese
4	cups diced cooked potatoes		

Cook bacon in skillet at 300° until crisp. Remove bacon and crumble when cool; reserve. Pour off excess drippings; reserving 2 tablespoons in skillet. Add mushrooms and green pepper; cook at 225° for 2 minutes. Stir in potatoes; cook until crisp, about 8 minutes, stirring occasionally. Pour eggs over potato mixture; cook until eggs are set, stirring occasionally. Stir in bacon; season to taste with salt and pepper. Sprinkle cheese over potato mixture; cook, covered, until cheese is melted, about 2 minutes.

6 servings

Cheesy Diced Potatoes

2 tablespoons butter	Salt and pepper
¾ cup chopped red pepper	¾ cup shredded Asiago cheese
½ cup sliced green onions	½ cup shredded sharp cheddar cheese
½ 32-oz. bag frozen Southern-Style Hash Brown Potatoes	

Heat butter in skillet at Warm until melted. Add red pepper and onions; stir-fry at 250° for 1 to 2 minutes. Stir in frozen potatoes. Cook, covered, at 300° for 10 minutes, turning occasionally. Uncover; cook, turning frequently until potatoes are golden, about 2 to 3 minutes. Season to taste with salt and pepper. Sprinkle cheeses over top. Cover; cook until cheese is melted, about 1 to 2 minutes.

Substitution Tip: *Substitute frozen O'Brian Potatoes for Southern-Style Hash Brown Potatoes. Omit red peppers and green onions.*

6 servings

Shredded Potato Bake

1 pound potatoes, peeled, shredded	½ teaspoon salt
1 small onion, finely chopped	⅛ teaspoon white pepper
¼ cup finely chopped green pepper	2 tablespoons vegetable oil
¼ cup all-purpose flour	Grated Parmesan cheese
2 eggs, beaten	Ground nutmeg

Mix potatoes, onion, green pepper, flour, eggs, salt, and pepper. Heat skillet at 225°. Add oil and potato mixture to skillet, shaping until round and flat with spatula; cook until golden brown on bottom, 10 to 12 minutes. Slide potato mixture onto dinner plate; invert into skillet; cook until bottom is brown and crisp, 10 to 15 minutes. Slide onto serving plate; sprinkle lightly with cheese and nutmeg. Cut into wedges to serve.

4 to 6 servings

Whole Wheat Pancakes with Blueberry Sauce

1⅓ cups all-purpose flour	¼ teaspoon ground nutmeg
⅔ cup whole wheat flour	2 cups milk
¼ cup sugar	¼ cup vegetable oil
4 teaspoons baking powder	2 eggs, beaten
1 teaspoon salt	Vegetable oil
1 teaspoon ground cinnamon	**Blueberry Sauce** (see recipe below)

Mix flours, sugar, baking powder, salt, cinnamon, and nutmeg in medium bowl. Beat milk, oil, and eggs in small bowl; mix into flour mixture until smooth. Heat skillet at 350°; brush bottom of skillet lightly with oil. Pour batter into skillet, using about 3 tablespoons batter for each pancake; cook until bubbles form on tops of pancakes and bottoms of pancakes are golden. Turn; cook until golden. Serve pancakes with Blueberry Sauce.

4 servings

Blueberry Sauce

½ cup butter or margarine	2 teaspoons grated lemon peel
2 tablespoons light brown sugar	1 16-ounce package frozen blueberries, thawed
¼ cup seedless red raspberry jam	
2 teaspoons lemon juice	

Heat butter in skillet at Warm until melted. Stir in sugar; cook 1 minute. Stir in jam, lemon juice, and lemon peel; cook 1 minute. Stir in blueberries; cook at 400° until slightly thickened, stirring constantly. Pour blueberry mixture into pitcher or bowl; place in small pan of hot water to keep warm.

About 3 cups

Vanilla Cream French Toast with Almond Syrup

1	loaf unsliced, day-old bread	1½	teaspoons ground cinnamon
1½	cups half-and-half or milk	1	teaspoon vanilla
3	eggs, beaten	6	tablespoons butter or margarine
2	tablespoons sugar		**Almond Syrup** (see recipe below)

Cut eight 1-inch thick slices from bread, reserving rest of loaf for other use.

Beat half-and-half and eggs in shallow bowl until smooth; mix in sugar, cinnamon, and vanilla. Heat 3 tablespoons butter in skillet at Warm until melted. Dip 4 bread slices into half-and-half mixture, coating both sides of bread generously with mixture; cook at 275° until golden, 3 to 4 minutes on each side. Remove French toast from skillet; keep warm. Repeat with remaining butter and bread slices. Serve with Almond Syrup.

4 servings

Almond Syrup

2	tablespoons butter or margarine	⅓	cup dark corn syrup
¾	cup slivered almonds	1 to 2	tablespoons lemon juice
2	cups light brown sugar	1	tablespoon grated lemon peel
¾	cup water		

Heat butter in skillet at Warm until melted. Add almonds; cook at 200° until almonds are golden. Remove almonds from skillet. Add sugar, water, corn syrup, lemon juice, and lemon peel; cook at 200° until sugar is dissolved and syrup is thickened to desired consistency, about 10 minutes. Stir in almonds. Pour syrup mixture into pitcher or bowl; place in small pan of hot water to keep warm.

About 1¾ cups

Cinnamon Apple Rings

2 tablespoons butter or margarine
1 tablespoon light brown sugar
⅛ teaspoon ground cinnamon

2 medium apples, cored, sliced
  into ¼-inch rings
¼ cup golden raisins

Heat butter in skillet at Warm until melted. Stir in sugar and cinnamon; cook 1 minute. Add apples and raisins; cook, covered, at 200° until apples are tender and glazed, about 2 minutes on each side.

6 servings

Honeyed Oranges and Grapefruit

1 cup orange juice
2 tablespoons honey
⅛ teaspoon ground cinnamon
⅛ teaspoon ground nutmeg

⅛ teaspoon ground allspice
3 medium oranges, peeled, sliced
1 large grapefruit, peeled, cut into
  segments

Mix orange juice, honey, cinnamon, nutmeg, and allspice in skillet; cook at 400° until boiling. Stir in oranges and grapefruit; simmer, between Warm and 200°, covered, 5 minutes. Spoon into serving bowl; serve warm or refrigerate, covered, until chilled; serve cold.

4 servings

Apricots in Orange Juice

2 7-ounce packages dried apricots
2 cups orange juice
1 to 2 tablespoons apricot preserves
1 cinnamon stick

2 whole allspice
1 whole clove
⅛ teaspoon ground mace

Combine all ingredients in skillet; heat at 400° until boiling. Reduce heat to simmer, between Warm and 200°; cook, covered, until apricots are tender, about 10 minutes. Spoon apricot mixture into serving bowl; let cool.

4 servings

Ginger Peach Chutney

2	cups apricot nectar	1	teaspoon minced fresh gingerroot
½	cup cider vinegar	1	teaspoon dry mustard
2½	pounds peaches, peeled, pitted, coarsely chopped	½	teaspoon ground cinnamon
		¼	teaspoon ground mace
1	cup raisins	½ to ¾	cup light brown sugar
⅓	cup finely chopped onion		

Combine all ingredients, except sugar, in skillet; cook at 400° until boiling, stirring occasionally. Reduce heat to simmer, between Warm and 200°. Stir in sugar to taste, stirring constantly until sugar is dissolved. Cook until thickened to desired consistency, stirring occasionally. Remove to bowl; cool to room temperature. Refrigerate, covered, up to 1 month.

About 3 cups

Cinnamon-Spice Apple Butter

8	cups coarsely chopped, cored, peeled tart apples	1 to 1¼	cups sugar
		½	teaspoon ground cinnamon
⅔	cup water	½	teaspoon ground allspice
2	tablespoons lemon juice	¼	teaspoon ground cloves

Combine apples, water, and lemon juice in skillet; cook at 400° until boiling. Reduce heat to simmer, between Warm and 200°. Cook, covered, until apples are tender, about 20 minutes. Stir in 1 cup sugar, cinnamon, allspice, and cloves; cook until thickened to desired consistency, 10 to 15 minutes, stirring frequently. Add remaining ¼ cup sugar, if necessary, for sweetness; cook, stirring until sugar is dissolved. Remove to bowl; cool to room temperature. Refrigerate, covered, up to 1 month.

2 cups

English Muffins

2	cups milk	1	¼-ounce package active dry yeast
3	tablespoons butter or margarine	4½ to 4¾	cups all-purpose flour
2	tablespoons sugar		Vegetable shortening
1½	teaspoons salt	1½	tablespoons cornmeal

Heat milk in skillet at 400° just until bubbles begin to appear. Turn heat to Off; stir in butter, sugar, and salt, stirring until butter is melted. Cool to lukewarm (110°). Stir in yeast until dissolved; let stand 2 minutes. Stir in enough flour to make moderately stiff dough; stirring until smooth, about 5 minutes. Let stand, covered, until dough has doubled in size, about 1 hour.

Remove dough from skillet. Clean skillet. Roll dough on lightly floured surface to ½-inch thickness; cut into 3-inch rounds with cutter. Let stand, lightly covered, 30 minutes (dough will not double in size).

Heat skillet at 250°. Grease skillet lightly with shortening and sprinkle with cornmeal; cook muffins in skillet until golden on bottom, about 15 minutes. Turn muffins; cook until golden on bottom, 15 to 20 minutes. Cool on wire rack. Split muffins with fork to serve.

12 to 14 muffins

Poppy Seed Pan Rolls

1	¼-ounce package active dry yeast	2	eggs
¼	cup warm milk (110°)	2½	cups all-purpose flour, divided
¼	cup warm water (110°)	¾	teaspoon salt
¼	cup butter or margarine, softened		Melted butter or margarine
2	tablespoons sugar		Poppy seed

Stir yeast into warm milk and water in small bowl; let stand 5 minutes.

Beat butter and sugar until fluffy in large bowl; beat in eggs, 1 at a time. Mix in 1 cup flour and salt. Mix in remaining 1½ cups flour alternately with yeast mixture, beating well after each addition (dough will be very soft and sticky). Spoon dough into 2 greased 6-cup muffin pans, filling each muffin cup half full. Brush tops of dough with melted butter; sprinkle lightly with poppy seed. Refrigerate 1 muffin pan, loosely covered with waxed paper.

Place remaining muffin pan on rack in skillet. Heat, covered, at Warm for 1 minute. Turn heat to Off; let stand, covered, until dough has doubled in size, 30 to 35 minutes. Heat skillet at 375°. Place muffin pan on rack; bake, covered, until deep golden on bottom, 22 to 25 minutes. Remove rolls from muffin pan; cool on wire rack. Turn heat to Off. Remove the other muffin pan from refrigerator when beginning to bake first pan; let stand at room temperature. When first pan of rolls is done, place other pan on rack in skillet. If skillet has cooled, heat, covered, at Warm for 1 minute. Turn heat to Off, let stand, covered, until dough has doubled in size, 45 to 55 minutes. Bake, covered, as above.

12 rolls

Oatmeal Loaves

2⅓	cups unbleached or bread flour	½	teaspoon salt
⅓	cup quick-cooking oats	¼	teaspoon baking soda
1	¼-ounce package active dry yeast	1¼	cups warm milk (120°)
2	teaspoons light brown sugar		

Mix flour, oats, yeast, sugar, salt, and baking soda in large bowl. Stir in milk; beat until mixture is smooth. Spoon batter into 2 greased loaf pans, 7½ x 3½ inches. Place loaf pans on rack in skillet. Heat, covered, at Warm for 1 minute. Turn heat to Off; let stand, covered, until batter has doubled in size, about 45 minutes.

Heat skillet at 325°. Bake, covered, until bottom of bread is deep golden and loaves sound hollow when tapped, 50 to 60 minutes. Remove loaves from pans; cool on wire rack.

2 loaves

Individual Brioche *(Rich Yeast Rolls)*

1	¼-ounce package active dry yeast	3 to 3¼	cups all-purpose flour, divided
¼	cup warm water (110°)	1½	teaspoons salt
⅓	cup butter or margarine, softened	¼	cup milk
2	tablespoons sugar	1	egg, beaten
2	eggs		

Stir yeast into warm water in small bowl; let stand 5 minutes. Beat butter and sugar in mixer bowl until fluffy; beat in 2 eggs; 1 at a time. Add 1 cup flour and salt; mix in milk and beat at medium speed for 2 minutes. Mix in enough remaining flour to make soft dough. Knead on lightly floured surface until dough is smooth and elastic, about 5 minutes. Place dough in greased casserole; turn greased side up. Place casserole on rack in skillet. Heat, covered, at Warm for 1 minute. Turn heat to Off; let stand until dough has doubled in size, 1 to 1½ hours.

Punch dough down. Shape two-thirds of the dough into 12 balls; place in 12 greased 6-ounce custard cups or two 6-cup muffin pans. Shape remaining one-third dough into 12 balls. Make holes in tops of larger balls with finger; place smaller balls in holes. Refrigerate 6 of the custard cups, loosely covered with waxed paper. Place remaining 6 custard cups on rack in skillet. Heat, covered, at Warm for 1 minute. Turn heat to Off. Let stand, covered, until dough has doubled in size, about 20 minutes; brush rolls lightly with beaten egg. Heat skillet at 375°, bake rolls, covered, until deep golden brown on bottom, 25 to 30 minutes. Remove rolls; cool on wire rack. Turn heat to Off.

Remove the other 6 custard cups from refrigerator when beginning to bake first rolls; let stand at room temperature. When first rolls are done, place other custard cups on rack in skillet. If skillet has cooled, heat, covered, at Warm for 1 minute. Turn heat to Off. Let stand, covered, until dough has doubled in size, 30 to 40 minutes. Bake, covered, as above.

12 rolls

Steamed Brown Bread

1	cup gingersnap crumbs		1	cup buttermilk
⅔	cup unbleached flour		⅓	cup dark molasses
⅔	cup whole wheat flour		¾	cup raisins
1	teaspoon baking powder		1	tablespoon grated orange peel
1	teaspoon baking soda			Water
½	teaspoon salt			

Mix gingersnaps, flours, baking powder, baking soda, and salt in medium bowl; mix in remaining ingredients, except water, until blended. Spoon batter into 2 greased 16-ounce cans. Cover cans firmly with double-thickness aluminum foil. Place rack in skillet; place cans on rack; add 1½ inches water. Heat skillet at 400° until boiling. Reduce heat to simmer, between Warm and 200°; cook, covered, until toothpicks inserted in centers of breads come out clean, 45 to 60 minutes. Cool on wire rack 5 minutes; remove from cans and cool completely.

2 breads

Silky Apricot Crêpes

	Crêpes (see recipe below)		¼	teaspoon almond extract
1½	cups whole milk ricotta cheese		¼	teaspoon ground cinnamon
¾	cup diced dried apricots		2	tablespoons butter
½	cup powdered sugar		¾	cup apricot syrup

Make Crêpes. Reserve.

Mix cheese, apricots, sugar, almond extract, and cinnamon in medium bowl. Spread approximately 1 rounded tablespoon of filling onto each crêpe. Fold in half, then in half again. Heat butter in skillet at Warm until melted. Add crêpes. Cook at 250° for 2 minutes. Turn crêpes and cook until heated through, 1 to 2 minutes. Serve warm with apricot syrup.

Crêpes

1	cup all-purpose flour		2	eggs, beaten
1	tablespoon sugar		2	tablespoons butter, melted
1	cup milk			

Combine flour and sugar in medium bowl. Whisk in milk, eggs, and butter until smooth. Let batter stand 15 minutes.

Heat skillet at 350°. Pour 2 tablespoons batter into skillet. Spread slightly to form a 5-inch crêpe. Cook until golden on the bottom, about 1 minute. Turn crêpe and cook 30 seconds. Remove from skillet. Repeat with remaining batter.

16 to 18 crêpes

Almond Cream Cheese Coffee Cake

1¾ cups plus 1 tablespoon all-purpose flour, divided	2 eggs, divided
¾ cup sugar, divided	½ teaspoon almond extract
½ teaspoon baking powder	1 8-ounce package cream cheese, softened
½ teaspoon baking soda	¼ cup firmly packed light brown sugar
¼ teaspoon salt	2 tablespoons butter, melted
½ cup chilled butter, cut into pieces	¼ teaspoon ground cinnamon
¾ cup sour cream	¼ cup toasted sliced almonds

Butter and flour 9-inch springform pan.

Combine 1½ cups flour, ½ cup sugar, baking powder, soda, and salt in medium bowl. Add chilled butter; using fingertips blend until mixture resembles coarse crumbs. Stir in sour cream, 1 egg, and almond extract until well combined. Spread batter evenly on bottom and about 2 inches up the side of prepared pan.

Beat cream cheese, remaining ¼ cup sugar, remaining egg, and 1 tablespoon flour until smooth in small bowl. Pour into center of batter in springform pan.

Combine remaining ¼ cup flour, brown sugar, butter, and cinnamon until mixture is crumbly. Sprinkle over cream cheese mixture. Sprinkle almonds over streusel.

Place springform pan on wire rack in preheated skillet at 400°. Bake, covered, for 1½ hours or until toothpick inserted into cake and filling comes out clean. Remove cake to cooling rack. Let stand 10 minutes. Carefully run a thin metal spatula around edge of pan; remove side of pan. Let cake cool on rack at least 1 hour before serving. Store any leftover cake in refrigerator.

12 servings

Appetizers

Whether your entertaining style is casual or elegant, you'll find the electric skillet to be a great social asset. Guests can't resist dipping crackers or chips into warm *Cheesy Artichoke Dip* or spicy *Chile Con Queso*, and nobody can stop at just one simmering *Meatball with Chili Sauce* or *Smoked Sausage Bite*. These appetizers are served right from the skillet, so they stay temptingly hot and tasty.

The electric skillet conveniently cooks while guests gather, adding the tantalizing aromas of *Chicken Wings Teriyaki* or *Tomato and Rosemary Focaccia* to the merriment of the party. *Stuffed Mushrooms* and *Curried Snack Mix* will entice all appetites. For something out-of-the-ordinary and delightfully delicious, try *Caramelized Onion and Cranberry Crostini*. This recipe will soon become an entertaining favorite.

Many of the recipes in this chapter can be prepared in advance or ingredients can be cut and arranged ahead of time, leaving the final cooking or reheating until later. This strategy enables you to spend your time welcoming guests and savoring the fun.

Stuffed Mushrooms

    36 fresh mushrooms
          Spinach or Cheese Stuffing (see recipes below)
          Dry bread crumbs

Remove stems from mushrooms; reserve 3 tablespoons finely chopped stems for stuffing (refrigerate remaining stems for other use).

Make desired stuffing. Fill each mushroom with teaspoon of stuffing. Dip mushrooms, stuffing sides down, in bread crumbs to coat stuffing. Arrange mushrooms, stuffing sides down, in skillet; cook, covered, at 200° for 5 minutes. Turn mushrooms over; cook, covered, until heated, about 5 minutes. Serve warm.

36 mushroom caps

Spinach Stuffing

1	slice bacon	3 tablespoons dry bread crumbs
3	tablespoons minced onion	¾ cup shredded sharp cheddar cheese
3	tablespoons finely chopped mushroom stems	¼ teaspoon salt
¾	cup frozen chopped spinach, thawed and squeezed dry	⅛ teaspoon ground nutmeg

Cook bacon in skillet at 300° until crisp. Remove bacon and crumble when cool. Add onion and mushroom stems; cook at 225° for 2 minutes. Stir in spinach; cook until heated, 1 to 2 minutes. Stir in bread crumbs; cook 1 minute. Turn skillet to Off; stir in cheese, bacon, salt, and nutmeg.

About ¾ cup

Cheese Stuffing

1	3-ounce package cream cheese, softened	3 tablespoons finely chopped mushroom stems
½	cup shredded Swiss cheese	2 tablespoons finely chopped walnuts
2	tablespoons crumbled blue cheese	

Beat cream cheese until smooth; mix in remaining ingredients.

About ¾ cup

Caramelized Onion and Cranberry Crostini

1 8-ounce package light cream
   cheese, softened
2 teaspoons chopped fresh thyme
¼ cup chopped walnuts
1 long baguette, cut into ½-inch slices
   Olive oil for brushing

2 tablespoons olive oil
4 cups slivered onions
½ teaspoon salt
½ cup dried cranberries or mixture
   of dried cranberries, cherries, raisins,
   and blueberries

Mix together cream cheese and thyme in small bowl. Refrigerate until ready to serve.

Heat skillet at 300°. Add walnuts; heat until toasted, about 8 to 10 minutes, stirring occasionally. Remove and reserve.

Brush both sides of each slice of bread with olive oil. Toast in skillet at 300° until golden on each side, 3 to 4 minutes per side. Reserve. Wipe any crumbs from skillet.

Heat olive oil in skillet. Add onions and salt; sauté until they begin to brown, about 15 minutes, stirring frequently. Reduce heat to 275°. Add cranberries; cook until onions are sweet and cranberries are softened, about 15 to 20 minutes. If skillet gets too dry, add 1 tablespoon water. Stir in walnuts. Remove and cool slightly or completely. Spread cream cheese equally among toasted bread slices. Top with onion-cranberry mixture.

Preparation Tip: To make onion slivers, cut onion in half crosswise then into thin wedges.

30 appetizers

Cheesy Artichoke Dip

⅓ cup sliced almonds
1 8-ounce package cream cheese,
   softened
¼ cup sour cream
¼ cup plain yogurt
2 tablespoons fresh lemon juice
½ tablespoon Dijon-style mustard
1 teaspoon Worcestershire sauce
1 clove garlic, minced

1 14-ounce can artichoke hearts,
   drained, chopped
1 10-ounce bag frozen chopped spinach,
   thawed and squeezed dry
1 green onion, finely chopped
½ cup grated Parmesan cheese
1 cup shredded mozzarella cheese
1 to 2 tablespoons hot pepper sauce, to taste
   Pita triangles, crackers, or vegetables

Heat skillet at 300°. Heat almonds until golden. Remove almonds; reserve.

Beat cream cheese, sour cream, yogurt, lemon juice, mustard, Worcestershire, and garlic in large bowl. Stir in artichokes, spinach, onion, cheeses, and hot pepper sauce. Transfer mixture to skillet; heat at Warm until cheese is melted, about 8 to 10 minutes, stirring occasionally. Top with reserved almonds. Serve with toasted pita triangles, crackers, or cut vegetables of choice.

4 generous cups

Tomato and Rosemary Focaccia

3	tablespoons olive oil, divided			Olive oil for brushing skillet and dough
1	cup sliced onions			
1	16-ounce package hot roll mix	½	cup seeded chopped tomatoes
1	tablespoon chopped fresh rosemary	½	cup shredded Italian blend cheese (mozzarella and other white cheeses)
1¼	cups warm water (120° to 130°)		
	Flour, as necessary for kneading dough	½ to 1	teaspoon coarse salt
		1	tablespoon fresh rosemary leaves

Heat 1 tablespoon olive oil in skillet at 225°. Sauté onions until limp, about 5 to 7 minutes, stirring often. Remove onions and reserve. Do not clean skillet.

On the hot roll mix package, follow the "pizza recipe" directions for mixing and kneading dough, adding rosemary to the contents of the box, increasing the water to 1¼ cups, adding the remaining 2 tablespoons oil and omitting the egg. If necessary add flour to dough during kneading to keep it from sticking to the surface and hands.

Brush oil on skillet to grease well, if necessary. Turn dough into skillet and cover; let rest 5 minutes. Pat dough out evenly in bottom of skillet using well-oiled hands. Cover; bake at 200° for 20 minutes. Increase temperature to 250°; bake for 10 minutes. Gently brush top with olive oil and carefully turn over. Brush bread with olive oil. Top with onions, tomatoes, cheese, and salt. Cover; cook until bread is baked through, about 15 to 18 minutes. Remove to cooling rack. Sprinkle with rosemary leaves.

Makes 1 loaf

Frittata Squares

7	eggs, beaten	½	teaspoon salt
1¾	cups shredded Swiss cheese	¼	teaspoon Worcestershire sauce
1¾	cups shredded cheddar cheese	¼	teaspoon hot pepper sauce
1	14-ounce can artichoke hearts, drained, sliced	⅛	teaspoon ground nutmeg
10	whole wheat crackers, finely crushed	⅛	teaspoon white pepper
1	teaspoon dried basil leaves	3	tablespoons butter or margarine
½	teaspoon grated lemon peel	1	cup sliced mushrooms
		¼	cup sliced green onions

Mix all ingredients except butter, mushrooms, and onions in large bowl. Heat butter in skillet at Warm until melted. Add mushrooms and onions; cook at 250° until onions are tender, about 2 minutes. Pour egg mixture into skillet, stirring gently to distribute mixture evenly over bottom of skillet; cook, covered, until egg mixture is set, 10 to 12 minutes. Cut into small squares with plastic or wooden utensil. Serve warm.

36 squares

Cheese Crisps

½   cup shredded cheddar cheese
½   cup shredded Swiss cheese
¼   cup butter or margarine, softened
¼   teaspoon Worcestershire sauce

¼   teaspoon salt
⅓   cup all-purpose flour
½   cup crispy rice cereal

Mix cheeses, butter, Worcestershire, and salt. Add flour and cereal; form dough mixture into log, 1 inch in diameter. Wrap in plastic wrap; place in freezer 30 minutes, or until ready to cook.

Heat skillet at 350°. Cut dough into ¼-inch slices; cook until browned on both sides, turning with plastic or wooden spatula. Serve warm or at room temperature.

24 appetizers

Sautéed Cheese Wedges

9   ounces Camembert or Brie cheese, well chilled
1   egg, beaten
    Dry bread crumbs

2   tablespoons butter or margarine
1   green onion, sliced
½   cup chutney
½   teaspoon prepared mustard

Cut cheese into 8 wedges. Dip cheese wedges in egg; coat generously with bread crumbs. Heat butter in skillet at Warm until melted. Add cheese; cook at 225° until cheese wedges are golden on all sides, turning carefully with tongs (cheese will become soft, but should not melt). Arrange cheese on serving plate.

Add green onion to skillet; cook 2 to 3 minutes. Stir in chutney and mustard; cook until bubbly, about 2 minutes. Spoon chutney mixture over cheese. Serve warm.

Preparation Tip: Chilled cheddar, brick, or mozzarella cheese may be substituted for the Camembert or Brie cheese; cut into 1-inch cubes or wedges.

4 servings

Nutty Beef Dip

1	2½-ounce jar dried beef, chopped	1	8-ounce package cream cheese, cubed
2	tablespoons butter or margarine	1	cup sour cream
½	cup chopped pecans	¼	cup mayonnaise
½	cup chopped almonds	½	teaspoon dried dillweed
¼	cup chopped onion		Assorted crackers
1	cup shredded brick cheese		

Rinse dried beef under warm water to rehydrate; drain well; reserve.

Heat butter in skillet at Warm until melted. Add nuts; cook at 250° for 2 minutes. Stir in onion; cook 2 minutes. Reduce heat to 200°. Add cheeses, sour cream, mayonnaise, and dillweed, stirring until cheeses are melted and mixture is heated. Stir in beef; cook 1 minute. Reduce heat to Warm. Serve from skillet with crackers as dippers.

About 2¾ cups

Meatballs with Chili Sauce

	Beef and Sausage Meatballs	1	tablespoon sugar
	(see recipe below)	2	teaspoons Worcestershire sauce
½	cup chopped onion	½	teaspoon ground cumin
½	cup chopped green pepper	½	teaspoon salt
2	14½-ounce cans diced tomatoes	¼	teaspoon ground oregano
¼	cup chili sauce		

Make Beef and Sausage Meatballs. Remove meatballs; pour off excess drippings, reserving 2 tablespoons in skillet. Add onion and pepper; cook at 325° until tender, 3 to 4 minutes. Add remaining ingredients; cook at 400° until boiling. Add meatballs; reduce heat to simmer, between Warm and 200°; cook until sauce is thickened, 10 to 15 minutes, stirring occasionally. Reduce heat to Warm; serve meatballs from skillet with toothpicks or cocktail forks.

24 meatballs

Beef and Sausage Meatballs

½	pound lean ground beef	½	teaspoon chili powder
½	pound pork sausage	1	small clove garlic, minced
¼	cup minced onion	½	teaspoon salt
½	teaspoon beef flavor instant bouillon	⅛	teaspoon pepper

Mix all ingredients until blended in medium bowl. Roll meat mixture into 24 meatballs. Arrange meatballs in skillet; cook at 350° until meatballs are browned on all sides, 5 to 8 minutes.

24 meatballs

Chile Con Queso

4	slices bacon		2	teaspoons Worcestershire sauce
1	small onion, finely chopped		1 to 2	teaspoons hot pepper sauce (optional)
1	medium green pepper, finely chopped		2	cups shredded brick cheese
1	4-ounce can chopped green chiles		2	cups shredded American cheese
1	tomato, chopped		½	cup whipping cream or half-and-half
1	tablespoon dried coriander leaves			Tortilla chips

Cook bacon in skillet at 300° until crisp. Remove bacon and crumble when cool. Pour off excess drippings, reserving 1 tablespoon in skillet. Add onion, green pepper, and chiles; cook at 225° until tender, 2 to 3 minutes. Stir in tomato, coriander, Worcestershire, and hot pepper sauce; cook, covered, 5 minutes. Reduce heat to Warm. Stir in cheeses and cream; cook, covered, until cheeses are melted, stirring occasionally. Sprinkle with bacon. Serve from skillet with tortilla chips as dippers.

About 3 cups

Potstickers

6	ounces lean ground beef or pork		¼	teaspoon ground ginger
1	cup shredded Chinese or green cabbage		⅛	teaspoon salt
¼	cup finely chopped celery		⅛	teaspoon pepper
1	tablespoon minced green onion		24	won ton or 6 egg roll wrappers
1	tablespoon soy sauce			Water
1	tablespoon cornstarch		2 to 4	tablespoons peanut or vegetable oil
			2	cups chicken broth
				Soy sauce

Combine ground beef, cabbage, celery, onion, soy sauce, cornstarch, ginger, salt, and pepper in large bowl. Cut won ton wrappers into 3-inch rounds with cutter. Spoon about 1½ teaspoons beef mixture on each won ton wrapper; brush edges with water. Fold wrappers in half and seal edges with tines of fork to make potstickers.

Heat skillet at 375°. Add 2 tablespoons oil and potstickers; cook until golden on bottoms, about 3 minutes. Turn potstickers. Add chicken broth; cook, covered, at simmer, between Warm and 200°, until potstickers are tender and broth has evaporated, about 10 minutes. Continue cooking, uncovered, until bottoms of potstickers are golden, adding more oil, if necessary. Serve hot with soy sauce.

24 appetizers

Smoked Sausage Bites

1	teaspoon vegetable oil	½	cup maple or pancake syrup
12	ounces smoked sausage, cut into ½-inch slices	¼	cup bourbon
¼	cup chopped onion	1	teaspoon prepared mustard
¾	cup chili sauce	¼	teaspoon pepper

Heat skillet at 300°. Add oil, sausage, and onion; cook until sausage is browned, 3 to 4 minutes. Stir in remaining ingredients; cook until hot and bubbly. Reduce heat to Warm. Serve sausage from skillet with toothpicks or cocktail forks.

6 to 8 servings

Pork Saté

¼	cup soy sauce	1	clove garlic
2	tablespoons dry sherry	½	teaspoon dried coriander leaves
2	tablespoons sugar	¼	cup red pepper flakes
½	teaspoon minced garlic	¼	cup water
½	teaspoon ground ginger	⅓	cup creamy peanut butter
1	pound boneless lean pork, cut into bite-size pieces	2	tablespoons vegetable oil
1	cup flaked coconut	1	small cucumber, thinly sliced
1¼	cups warm water (120°)	1	small onion, thinly sliced
⅓	cup chopped onion		Rice wine vinegar or distilled white vinegar

Mix soy sauce, sherry, sugar, minced garlic, and ginger in small bowl; pour over pork pieces in shallow glass baking dish, stirring to coat pieces evenly. Let stand 30 minutes. Remove pork from marinade; discard marinade.

Place coconut and warm water in food processor or blender; process until smooth, 1 to 2 minutes. Strain mixture into skillet, discarding coconut. Place onion, garlic clove, coriander, red pepper, and water in food processor or blender; process until smooth, about 1 minute. Stir into mixture in skillet. Heat at 400° until mixture is boiling. Reduce heat to simmer, between Warm and 200°; cook 4 minutes, stirring frequently. Stir in peanut butter; cook until mixture thickens, 1 to 2 minutes, stirring constantly. Pour into serving bowl; keep warm. Clean skillet.

Heat skillet at 325°. Add oil and pork; cook until meat is brown, 2 to 3 minutes, stirring constantly. Transfer meat to another serving bowl.

Place cucumber and onion in small bowl; sprinkle with vinegar and toss to coat lightly. Serve meat with peanut butter sauce for dipping. Garnish with cucumber mixture.

4 servings

Chicken Wings Teriyaki

⅔	cup teriyaki sauce	1½	teaspoons minced fresh gingerroot
½	cup water	1	clove garlic, minced
⅓	cup dry sherry	2	pounds chicken wings, tips cut off
2	tablespoons rice wine vinegar or distilled white vinegar	2	tablespoons vegetable oil
⅓	cup light brown sugar	1½	tablespoons cornstarch
		3	tablespoons cold water

Mix teriyaki sauce, water, sherry, vinegar, sugar, gingerroot, and garlic in shallow glass baking dish; add chicken. Refrigerate, covered, 1 to 4 hours, turning chicken occasionally.

Remove chicken from marinade; reserve marinade. Heat skillet at 325°. Add oil and chicken; cook, covered, until tender and golden, 5 to 8 minutes, turning once. Remove chicken; keep warm.

Add reserved marinade to skillet; cook at 400° until boiling. Mix cornstarch and cold water; stir into marinade. Reduce heat to 225°; cook until thickened, stirring constantly. Spoon sauce over chicken or serve in a bowl as a dipping sauce.

8 servings

Chicken and Vegetable Quesadillas

2	boneless skinless chicken breast halves	1	cup shredded jalapeño jack cheese
8	flour tortillas (7-inch diameter)	½	cup cooked and drained corn
½	cup chunky salsa	½	cup chopped green pepper
			Additional salsa, as desired

Pound chicken breasts lightly to an even ½-inch thickness. Heat skillet at 300°. Add chicken; cook until it springs back when touched, 9 to 11 minutes, turning every 3 minutes. Allow chicken to cool, chop into bite-size pieces.

Spread 2 tablespoons salsa over one side of each of 4 tortillas. Sprinkle each with ¼ cup chicken, ¼ cup cheese, 2 tablespoons corn, and 2 tablespoons green pepper. Cover each with another tortilla.

Spray skillet with nonstick cooking spray. Heat at 325°. Cook one quesadilla at a time, about 2 minutes per side or until golden and crisp. Cut each into 4 wedges. Serve with additional salsa.

4 servings

Curried Snack Mix

3	tablespoons butter or margarine	1	cup cashews
1½	tablespoons light brown sugar	1	cup cocktail peanuts
1½	teaspoons curry powder	½	cup shredded coconut
2	cups toasted wheat cereal squares	1	cup raisins

Heat butter in skillet at Warm until melted. Stir in sugar and curry powder; cook at 250° for 1 minute. Stir in cereal, cashews, and peanuts; cook at 275° for 5 minutes, stirring frequently. Add coconut; cook until mixture is golden, about 5 minutes, stirring frequently. Stir in raisins. Spread mixture on jelly roll pan to cool. Store in airtight container.

About 5 cups

Popcorn Snack Mix

2	tablespoons vegetable oil	¾	teaspoon dried oregano leaves
⅓	cup popcorn	1	cup mixed nuts
1	tablespoon butter or margarine	½	cup grated Parmesan cheese

Heat skillet at 350°. Add oil and popcorn; heat, covered, until corn is popped, shaking pan gently after corn begins to pop. Place popped corn in large bowl.

Heat butter in skillet at Warm until melted. Stir in oregano and nuts; cook at 275° until nuts are golden, about 5 minutes. Combine nuts and popped corn. Sprinkle with cheese; toss.

About 5 cups

Vegetables & Side Dishes

Think of your electric skillet as a guardian of good nutrition. Combine the skillet's performance and versatility with a brilliant variety of flavors and accompaniments, and watch how vegetables and side dishes can transform into everyday meal highlights.

Carrots and Parsnips as well as *Green Beans with Blue Cheese and Toasted Pecans* turn ordinary vegetables into noteworthy additions to your meal repertoire. Vegetables that are often overlooked will surprise and delight you with *Mediterranian-Style Artichoke Hearts* and *Zucchini and Eggplant Sauté.* There are also many dishes that would otherwise bake in an oven, such as *Jalapeño Corn Cakes, Waldorf Baked Squash,* and *Summer Vegetable Frittata,* that are made in the moist heat of a skillet with even better results.

Nothing could be easier than skillet rice combinations with *Toasted Pecan Rice* and *Fruit and Nut Rice.* We've even added delightful side dish classics like *Pasta with Roasted Garlic Tomato Sauce, New England Bean Bake,* and *Fruit and Sausage Stuffing,* each a joy to savor and serve.

There are many wonderful recipes in this mix of vegetables and side dishes. All of them reveal just how wonderful "good-for-you" foods can taste.

Carrots and Parsnips

2	tablespoons olive oil		⅓	cup vegetable or chicken broth, or water
2	tablespoons unsalted butter		1	teaspoon finely chopped fresh
¾	pound parsnips, peeled, cut into ½-inch dice			rosemary or ¼ teaspoon dried
¾	pound medium carrots, peeled, cut into ½-inch dice		1 to 2	teaspoons fresh lemon juice
			2	tablespoons finely chopped fresh flat-leaf parsley
2	cloves garlic, minced			Salt and pepper

Heat oil and butter at Warm until butter is melted. Add parsnips; cook at 350° for 5 minutes, stirring occasionally. Add carrots; cook until parsnips and carrots are brown and almost tender, about 5 to 8 minutes, stirring occasionally. Add garlic; stir-fry 30 seconds. Reduce heat to 200°. Add broth and rosemary; simmer, covered, until vegetables are just tender, about 3 minutes. Uncover. Increase heat to 275°; boil until liquid is evaporated. Stir in lemon juice, parsley, and salt and pepper to taste.

4 servings

Mustard Glazed Carrots

1	10-ounce package frozen carrots		2	teaspoons lemon juice
2	cups water		½	teaspoon salt
2	tablespoons butter or margarine		⅛	teaspoon white pepper
1	tablespoon honey		1	teaspoon minced parsley
2	teaspoons Dijon-style mustard			

Place carrots in small bowl; place on rack in skillet. Add water to skillet; cook, covered, 8 to 10 minutes. Remove carrots from skillet and drain. Pour water from skillet.

Add butter to skillet; heat at Warm until melted. Stir in honey, mustard, lemon juice, salt, and pepper; cook 1 minute. Stir in carrots; cook, covered, at 200° until heated through, about 1 minute. Sprinkle with parsley.

3 servings

Green Beans with Blue Cheese and Toasted Pecans

3	tablespoons unsalted butter, divided	1	pound fresh green beans, trimmed
⅓	cup pecans	⅓	cup reduced-sodium chicken or
¼	teaspoon cayenne pepper		vegetable broth
1	shallot, minced	¼	cup crumbled blue cheese
1	garlic clove, minced	1 to 2	teaspoons fresh lemon juice

Heat 1 tablespoon butter in skillet at Warm until melted. Add pecans, sprinkle with cayenne pepper. Heat at 300° until toasted, about 2 to 3 minutes. Remove; coarsely chop when cool. Reserve.

Reduce heat to 200°. Add remaining 2 tablespoons butter, shallot, and garlic. Sauté until tender, about 2 minutes. Add green beans, stirring to coat with butter. Add broth; cover and simmer until liquid evaporates and beans are crisp-tender, about 7 to 9 minutes. Toss with lemon juice. Sprinkle with blue cheese and reserved pecans. Toss to warm slightly.

4 servings

Greek-Style Green Beans

2	tablespoons olive oil	2	14½-ounce cans diced tomatoes
1	pound fresh green beans, trimmed	1	tablespoon fresh thyme leaves or
¾	cup chopped onion		1 teaspoon dried
2	cloves garlic, minced		

Heat skillet at 225°. Add oil, beans, onion, and garlic; cook 7 minutes, stirring occasionally. Add tomatoes and thyme; cook, covered, until beans are tender, about 20 to 25 minutes.

6 to 8 servings

Italian-Style Broccoli

2	tablespoons pine nuts or slivered almonds	2	cups frozen sliced broccoli, thawed
2	tablespoons olive or vegetable oil	1	clove garlic, minced
			Salt and pepper

Heat skillet at 300°. Add pine nuts, heat until toasted, about 2 to 3 minutes. Remove and reserve.

Reduce heat to 225°. Add oil, broccoli, and garlic; cook until broccoli is crisp-tender and beginning to brown, about 4 minutes, stirring occasionally. Stir in reserved pine nuts; season to taste with salt and pepper.

2 servings

Braised Spicy Cauliflower

½	cup reduced-sodium chicken broth		½	teaspoon honey
2	tablespoons dry sherry		2	tablespoons peanut or vegetable oil
2	tablespoons tamari or soy sauce		1	head cauliflower, broken or cut
1	tablespoon hot chili paste (such as sambal olek)			into florets
1	tablespoon cider vinegar		3	green onions, finely chopped
2	teaspoons sesame oil		2	tablespoons minced fresh gingerroot
			3	garlic cloves, minced

Mix broth, sherry, tamari, chili paste, vinegar, sesame oil, and honey in small bowl. Reserve.

Heat skillet at 400°. Add oil; when heated stir in cauliflower to coat with oil. Stir in onions, ginger, cloves, and reserved broth mixture. Continue to cook for 3 minutes. Reduce heat to 225°. Cover and let braise until just tender, 10 to 12 minutes.

Shopping Tip: Sambal olek is found in the Asian foods section of the supermarket and at Asian markets.

4 to 6 servings

Sautéed Balsamic Tomatoes

2	teaspoons olive oil		1	tablespoon chopped fresh oregano
2	pints grape or cherry tomatoes			Salt and pepper
1½	tablespoons balsamic vinegar			

Heat skillet at 225°. Add oil and tomatoes; cook until tomatoes just begin to break. Add vinegar; toss to coat. Cook until vinegar is reduced by half, about 2 to 3 minutes. Toss in oregano. Season to taste with salt and pepper. Serve warm, at room temperature, or cold.

4 to 6 servings

Grilled Tomato Slices

¼	cup butter or margarine		⅛	teaspoon dried tarragon leaves
½	cup dry bread crumbs		⅛	teaspoon dried sage leaves
¼	teaspoon salt		3	medium tomatoes, cut into ½-inch slices

Heat butter in skillet at Warm until melted. Stir in bread crumbs, salt, tarragon, and sage; cook at 200° until crumbs are browned, about 2 minutes. Add tomato slices; spoon crumb mixture over slices. Cook, covered, until tomatoes are heated, about 2 minutes.

6 servings

Jalapeño Corn Cakes

1	cup all-purpose flour	½	cup milk
½	cup cornmeal	1	cup shredded sharp cheddar cheese
¼	cup sugar	½	cup frozen whole kernel corn, thawed
1	tablespoon baking powder	1 to 2	tablespoons seeded finely chopped
¾	teaspoon salt		jalapeño pepper
⅓	cup chilled unsalted butter, cut into small pieces		Tomatillo salsa (salsa verde)

Mix flour, cornmeal, sugar, baking powder, and salt in medium bowl. Add butter; using fingertips blend mixture until crumbly. Add milk; stir until just blended with flour mixture. Stir in cheese, corn, and pepper.

Spray skillet with nonstick cooking spray. Heat at 275°. Drop batter in ⅓ cup amounts into skillet. Cover and cook until a toothpick inserted into corn cakes comes out clean, about 18 to 20 minutes. Serve warm with salsa as desired.

8 cakes

Baked Corn Custard

3	eggs, beaten	¼	teaspoon pepper
2	cups half-and-half	¼	teaspoon ground nutmeg
1	tablespoon butter or margarine, melted	1	15- to 16-ounce can whole kernel corn, drained
¼	cup all-purpose flour	1	cup shredded cheddar cheese
1	teaspoon sugar	¼	cup thinly sliced green onions
½	teaspoon dried savory leaves	1	tablespoon butter or margarine
½	teaspoon salt		

Whisk eggs, half-and-half, and melted butter in large bowl. Stir in flour, sugar, savory, salt, pepper, and nutmeg. Mix in corn, cheese, and onions.

Heat butter in skillet at Warm until melted. Pour in corn mixture; cook, covered, at 250° until set, about 30 minutes. Cut into squares with plastic or wooden utensil. Serve immediately.

8 servings

Mediterranean-Style Artichoke Hearts

2	tablespoons olive oil	¼	cup pitted kalamata olives
¼	cup chopped red onion	1	teaspoon fresh thyme leaves or
½	medium red pepper, cut into		½ teaspoon dried
	¼-inch strips	1	14-ounce can artichoke hearts,
1	small zucchini, cut into		drained, cut in half
	¼-inch slices		Salt and pepper
2	cups baby spinach	⅓	cup crumbled goat cheese

Heat oil in skillet at 225°. Add onion; sauté about 2 minutes. Add pepper and zucchini; sauté until tender, about 2 minutes. Toss in spinach, olives, and thyme; cook until spinach is just wilted, about 1 minute. Stir in artichoke hearts; heat through. Season to taste with salt and pepper. Sprinkle with cheese.

4 servings

Artichokes with Garlic Sauce

4	artichokes		Water
2	tablespoons olive or vegetable oil	½	cup butter or margarine
	Salt	3	cloves garlic, minced

Cut stems off artichokes; cut pointed tips off leaves with scissors. Stand artichokes in skillet; drizzle olive oil over artichokes and sprinkle with salt. Add 1 inch water to skillet; cook at 400° until boiling. Reduce heat to simmer, between Warm and 200°; cook, covered, until artichokes are tender (leaf will pull easily from base of artichoke), about 35 minutes. Cook, uncovered, until water has evaporated from skillet and artichokes are deep golden brown on the bottom, about 10 minutes. Remove artichokes; keep warm. Clean skillet.

Heat butter in skillet at 225° until melted. Add garlic; sauté 1 minute. Serve warm sauce over artichokes.

4 servings

Sautéed Asparagus with Garlic

1	pound fresh asparagus, ends trimmed	2	tablespoons water
1	clove garlic, minced		Salt
2	tablespoons olive or vegetable oil		

Place asparagus and garlic in skillet. Drizzle with oil and water; cook, covered, at 225° for 5 minutes. Reduce heat to 200°; cook until water has evaporated and asparagus is browned on all sides, 8 to 10 minutes, turning frequently with tongs. Season to taste with salt.

4 servings

Sugar-Glazed Brussels Sprouts and Onions

1	10-ounce package frozen Brussels sprouts	2	tablespoons sugar
1	cup water	1	16-ounce jar boiled whole onions
¼	teaspoon salt	¼	cup coarsely chopped walnuts
2	tablespoons butter or margarine		Salt and pepper

Heat skillet at 400°. Add Brussels sprouts, water, and salt; cook until boiling. Reduce heat to simmer, between Warm and 200°; cook, covered, until sprouts are tender, about 10 minutes. Remove sprouts from skillet; discard cooking liquid. Heat butter in skillet until melted. Add sugar; cook at 250° for 1 minute. Add onions; cook at 400° until onions are glazed, about 3 minutes, stirring frequently. Stir in sprouts and walnuts; cook 2 minutes. Season to taste with salt and pepper.

4 to 6 servings

Julienne Celery with Walnuts

4	ribs celery, cut crosswise into 3-inch pieces	1	teaspoon grated lemon peel
1	tablespoon butter or margarine	1	teaspoon lemon juice
1	tablespoon vegetable oil	¼	teaspoon salt
½	cup coarsely chopped walnuts	⅛	teaspoon pepper

Cut celery pieces lengthwise into ¼-inch strips. Heat butter and oil in skillet at Warm until butter is melted. Add walnuts; cook at 225° until browned, stirring frequently. Add celery and lemon peel; cook until crisp-tender, about 4 minutes, stirring occasionally. Sprinkle with lemon juice, salt, and pepper; toss.

4 servings

Spinach Salad with Sweet-Sour Dressing

6 slices bacon	1 small red onion, thinly sliced
6 cups fresh spinach, torn into bite-size pieces	1 cup sliced mushrooms
	Sweet-Sour Dressing (see recipe below)

Cook bacon in skillet at 300° until crisp. Remove bacon and crumble when cool; reserve. Clean skillet.

Make Sweet-Sour Dressing. Combine spinach, onion, and mushrooms in salad bowl. Spoon Sweet-Sour dressing over salad and toss. Sprinkle with reserved bacon.

6 servings

Sweet-Sour Dressing

¾ cup sugar	½ cup milk
1 tablespoon cornstarch	1 egg, beaten
¼ teaspoon salt	1 tablespoon butter or margarine
¼ cup distilled white vinegar	

Mix sugar, cornstarch, and salt in skillet. Stir in vinegar; cook at 400° until boiling, stirring constantly. Reduce heat to simmer, between Warm and 200°. Add milk and egg; cook until smooth and thickened, stirring constantly. Turn heat to Off; stir in butter until melted. Refrigerate, covered, until chilled, about 1 hour.

About 1½ cups

Wilted Spinach

12 slices bacon	1 tablespoon Worcestershire sauce
¾ cup tarragon vinegar	1½ teaspoons prepared mustard
⅓ cup brandy	2 10-ounce packages fresh spinach, washed, torn into bite-size pieces
⅓ cup sugar	

Cook bacon in skillet at 300° until crisp. Remove bacon and crumble when cool; reserve. Pour off excess drippings, reserving 1 tablespoon in skillet.

Add vinegar, brandy, sugar, Worcestershire, and mustard to drippings in skillet; cook until mixture begins to boil. Stir in spinach and reserved bacon; cook, covered, just until spinach is wilted, about 2 minutes. Serve immediately.

4 to 6 servings

Summer Vegetable Frittata

6 eggs, beaten	1 tablespoon olive oil
2 tablespoons chopped fresh basil	3 slices bacon, finely chopped
1 tablespoon chopped fresh parsley	2 cups coarsely chopped zucchini
1 teaspoon salt	1 cup coarsely chopped red pepper
1 teaspoon freshly ground pepper	1 5- to 6-ounce bag baby spinach, chopped
4 ounces feta cheese, crumbled, divided	

Whisk eggs, basil, parsley, salt, and pepper in medium bowl. Stir in half of the cheese. Reserve.

Heat skillet at 225°. Add oil and bacon; cook until edges begin to crisp, stirring frequently. Add zucchini and red pepper; cook until tender, about 5 minutes, stirring occasionally. Add spinach; cook, covered, just until wilted, about 1 to 2 minutes. Uncover. Stir in egg mixture distributing evenly with vegetables. Cook, until sides set, about 7 minutes, occasionally loosening sides with spatula. Sprinkle with remaining feta cheese. Cook, covered, until set, about 7 to 9 minutes.

6 servings

Beets in Orange Sauce

Orange Sauce (see recipe below)	1 small orange, peeled, sliced
2 15-ounce cans sliced beets, drained	½ cup coarsely chopped pecans

Make Orange Sauce. Stir beets into sauce in skillet. Cut orange slices into fourths. Stir in orange pieces and pecans; cook, covered, at 200° until beets are heated, about 3 minutes.

4 to 6 servings

Orange Sauce

⅔ cup water	½ teaspoon grated lemon peel
½ cup undiluted frozen orange juice concentrate, thawed	1 tablespoon cornstarch
¼ teaspoon chicken flavor instant bouillon	2 tablespoons cold water
½ teaspoon grated orange peel	2 tablespoons butter, softened
	¼ teaspoon pepper

Mix water, orange juice concentrate, bouillon, orange peel, and lemon peel in skillet; cook at 400° until boiling. Reduce heat to simmer, between Warm and 200°. Mix cornstarch and cold water; whisk into orange juice mixture until thickened, whisking constantly. Whisk in butter, 1 tablespoon at a time, until melted. Whisk in pepper.

Serving Tip: This recipe can be served with vegetables, chicken, pork, or ham. It can also be used as a dessert sauce by omitting bouillon and pepper.

1 cup

Asian Bean Sprout Salad

1	teaspoon sesame seeds	2	tablespoons sugar
1	tablespoon sesame or vegetable oil	¼	teaspoon ground ginger
2	tablespoons sliced green onions	3½	cups fresh bean sprouts
1	clove garlic, minced	1	cup thinly sliced celery
¼	cup rice wine vinegar	½	cup diagonally sliced carrot
2	teaspoons soy sauce		Shredded lettuce

Heat skillet at 225°. Add sesame seeds, heat until golden, stirring frequently. Remove sesame seeds; reserve.

Reduce heat to 200°. Add oil, onions, and garlic; cook 3 minutes. Stir in vinegar, soy sauce, sugar, and ginger; cook until heated, stirring constantly. Add bean sprouts, celery, and carrot. Spoon onto lettuce on serving plates; sprinkle with reserved sesame seeds.

Substitution Tip: Two cans (14 to 16 ounces each) bean sprouts may be substituted for the fresh. Drain bean sprouts and soak in ice water 1 hour to crisp.

6 servings

Mixed Vegetable Curry

3	tablespoons olive or vegetable oil	1	large potato, peeled, cut into ½-inch cubes
½	cup chopped onion		
1	clove garlic, minced	4	ounces green beans, cut into 1½-inch lengths
1	tablespoon curry powder		
½	teaspoon ground cumin	2	large carrots, cut diagonally into ¼-inch slices
½	teaspoon coriander seed or ¼ teaspoon ground coriander		
		⅓ to ½	cup water
¼	teaspoon ground cinnamon	¼	cup raisins
¼	teaspoon ground ginger	¼	cup frozen peas, thawed
⅛	teaspoon cayenne pepper		Salt
1	small head cauliflower (about 12 ounces) cut into florets		

Heat skillet at 225°. Add oil, onion, garlic, curry, cumin, coriander, cinnamon, ginger, and cayenne pepper; stir-fry 2 minutes. Add cauliflower, potato, beans, and carrots; stir-fry 4 minutes. Add ⅓ cup water; cook, covered, until vegetables are crisp-tender; about 4 minutes, adding more water, if necessary. Stir in raisins and peas; cook until heated, about 2 minutes, stirring constantly. Season to taste with salt.

6 servings

Antipasto Vegetable Salad

½ pound fresh asparagus, cut
   diagonally into 1-inch pieces
1 small zucchini, scored, cut into
   ¼-inch slices
2 medium carrots, cut into
   julienne strips

1 rib celery, cut into ¼-inch slices
   Water
   Tarragon dressing (see recipe below)
2 ounces brick cheese, cut into
   julienne strips
   Lettuce leaves

Place vegetables in vegetable steamer; place steamer in skillet. Add ½-inch water to skillet; cook, covered, at 400° until boiling. Reduce heat to simmer, between Warm and 200°; cook, covered, until vegetables are crisp-tender, 3 to 5 minutes. Remove vegetables and keep warm; discard water.

Make Tarragon Dressing. Pour over vegetables and toss. Serve warm or refrigerate until chilled. Add cheese; toss before serving. Serve on lettuce leaves.

Substitution Tip: Thawed frozen asparagus may be substituted for the fresh asparagus.

4 servings

Tarragon Dressing

3 tablespoons olive oil
3 tablespoons vegetable oil
1 clove garlic, minced
¼ cup white wine vinegar
1 tablespoon finely chopped onion

½ teaspoon Dijon-style mustard
½ teaspoon dried tarragon leaves
½ teaspoon salt
⅛ teaspoon pepper

Heat skillet at 225°. Add oils and garlic; cook 1 minute, stirring constantly. Stir in remaining ingredients; cook at 200° until simmering.

About ¾ cup

Steamed Vegetable Platter

2 cups chicken broth	1 medium sweet potato, cut into ¾-inch slices
1 bay leaf	2 celery hearts, trimmed
½ teaspoon dried thyme leaves	1 9-ounce package frozen artichoke hearts, thawed
½ teaspoon dried marjoram leaves	8 ounces green beans
½ teaspoon dried rosemary leaves	Salt and pepper
4 medium carrots, cut diagonally into 2-inch pieces	**Tarragon Chive Butter Sauce** (see recipe below)
2 medium potatoes, peeled, cut into halves	

Heat chicken broth, bay leaf, thyme, marjoram, and rosemary in skillet at 400° until boiling. Reduce heat to simmer, between Warm and 200°. Place carrots, potatoes, and celery hearts on rack in skillet; cook, covered, until vegetables are crisp-tender, about 25 minutes. Add artichoke hearts and green beans during last 10 minutes of cooking. Sprinkle vegetables lightly with salt and pepper. Arrange vegetables on serving platter; keep warm. Discard broth mixture. Clean skillet.

Make Tarragon Chive Butter Sauce. Serve over vegetables.

8 servings

Tarragon Chive Butter Sauce

⅓ cup butter or margarine	1 teaspoon dried chives
2 tablespoons all-purpose flour	½ teaspoon dried tarragon leaves
1 cup boiling water	½ teaspoon salt
1 to 2 tablespoons lemon juice	⅛ teaspoon white pepper
¼ teaspoon Dijon-style mustard	

Heat butter in skillet at Warm until melted. Stir in flour; cook 1 minute. Whisk in boiling water; cook at 200° until slightly thickened, about 5 minutes, whisking constantly. Whisk in lemon juice, mustard, chives, tarragon, salt, and pepper.

Serving Tip: This recipe can also be used with fish and seafood.

About 1¼ cups

Ratatouille

- 1 eggplant (about 1 pound), peeled, cut crosswise into ½-inch slices
  Salt
- 3 tablespoons olive oil
- 1 large onion, sliced
- 2 cloves garlic, minced
- 1 large green pepper, cut into ¼-inch strips
- 1 medium zucchini, cut into ½-inch slices
- 1 28-ounce can diced Italian plum tomatoes
- ¼ cup sliced black olives
- 1½ teaspoons dried basil leaves
- 1 teaspoon dried tarragon leaves
- ½ teaspoon salt
- ¼ teaspoon dried oregano leaves

Cut eggplant slices into quarters; sprinkle lightly with salt and let stand 30 minutes. Rinse well with cold water; drain thoroughly.

Heat skillet at 225°. Add oil, onion, and garlic; cook 2 minutes. Add green pepper; cook 1 minute. Add eggplant and remaining ingredients; cook at 400° until boiling. Reduce heat to simmer, between Warm and 200°; cook, covered, until eggplant is tender and mixture is desired consistency, 1 to 1½ hours.

6 to 8 servings

Zucchini and Eggplant Sauté

- 2 tablespoons olive oil
- 1 small onion, chopped
- 2 garlic cloves, minced
- 2 small zucchini, cut in half lengthwise, then in ¼-inch slices (1½ to 2 cups)
- 1 small eggplant, cut into ½-inch dice (1½ to 2 cups)
- ½ cup chicken or vegetable broth
- ½ teaspoon crushed red pepper
  Salt and pepper
- ¼ cup grated fontina cheese

Heat olive oil in skillet at 225°. Add onion and garlic; sauté 1 minute. Stir in zucchini and eggplant; sauté 3 minutes. Pour in broth; cook, covered, until vegetables are tender, about 3 to 5 minutes. Season to taste with red pepper, salt, and pepper. Sprinkle with cheese. Stir to blend. Serve warm.

4 servings

Waldorf Baked Squash

2	medium acorn squash	½	cup coarsely chopped walnuts
	Water	½	teaspoon ground cinnamon
1	cup coarsely chopped mixed	⅛	teaspoon ground nutmeg
	dried fruit	¼	cup maple syrup
½	cup chopped cored apple		

Cut squash into halves; remove seeds and discard. Place squash halves, cut sides down, on rack in skillet. Add 1 inch water; cook at 400° until boiling. Reduce heat to simmer, between Warm and 200°; cook, covered, until squash are tender, 35 to 40 minutes.

Mix dried fruit, apple, walnuts, cinnamon, and nutmeg in small bowl. Turn squash halves over, cut sides up, on rack; fill cavities with fruit mixture. Drizzle syrup over fruit mixture; cook, covered, until apple is tender, about 10 minutes.

4 servings

Stir-Fried Peppers and Squash

2	tablespoons vegetable oil	1	large yellow squash, cut into
½	cup chopped onion		pieces, 1½ x ¼ x ¼-inch
1	clove garlic, minced	½	teaspoon dried basil leaves
1	cup sliced mushrooms	½	teaspoon dried rosemary leaves
1	medium green pepper, cut into	½	teaspoon dried marjoram leaves
	¼-inch strips	¼	teaspoon dried thyme leaves
1	medium red pepper, cut into	1	large tomato, chopped
	¼-inch strips		Salt and pepper

Heat skillet at 225°. Add oil, onion, and garlic; cook 1 minute. Add mushrooms; stir-fry 1 minute. Add peppers; stir-fry 2 minutes. Add squash, basil, rosemary, marjoram, and thyme; stir-fry until vegetables are crisp-tender, 2 to 3 minutes. Stir in tomato; cook 1 minute. Season to taste with salt and pepper.

4 servings

Mixed Squash Sauté

6	slices bacon	1	medium zucchini, sliced
½	cup chopped onion	1	cup sliced mushrooms
1	clove garlic, minced	2 to 3	teaspoons Worcestershire sauce
1	medium yellow squash, sliced	¼	teaspoon salt

Cook bacon in skillet at 300° until crisp. Remove bacon and crumble when cool. Pour off excess drippings, reserving 2 tablespoons in skillet. Add onion and garlic; cook at 225° until tender, about 2 minutes. Stir in squash and mushrooms; cook until squash is tender, about 5 minutes, stirring frequently. Sprinkle with Worcestershire and salt; toss. Sprinkle with crumbled bacon.

6 servings

Glazed Sweet Potatoes

¼	cup coarsely chopped pecans	2	tablespoons bourbon
⅓	cup butter or margarine	1	tablespoon grated orange peel
½	cup packed light brown sugar	2	17-ounce cans sweet potatoes, drained

Heat skillet at 300°. Add pecans; heat until toasted, about 2 to 3 minutes. Remove and reserve.

Heat butter in skillet at Warm until melted. Add sugar, bourbon, and orange peel, stir until sugar is dissolved. Add potatoes, tossing to coat evenly with sugar syrup; cook, covered, at 250° until heated, about 8 minutes, stirring occasionally. Stir in reserved pecans.

Substitution Tip: Brandy or orange juice may be substituted for the bourbon.

6 servings

Sweet Potatoes with Nut Butter

1	tablespoon finely chopped pecans	⅛	teaspoon ground cinnamon
2	sweet potatoes	⅛	teaspoon ground nutmeg
	Vegetable oil	½	teaspoon grated orange peel
¼	cup butter or margarine, softened		

Heat skillet at 300°. Add pecans; heat until toasted, about 2 minutes. Remove and reserve.

Pierce potatoes in several places with fork; rub lightly with oil. Place potatoes on rack in skillet; cook, covered, at 375° until tender, about 45 minutes. Remove from skillet.

Beat butter, cinnamon, and nutmeg in small bowl until fluffy; mix in orange peel and reserved pecans. Serve on sweet potatoes.

2 servings

German Potato Salad

1½	pounds potatoes, peeled, cut into quarters	¾	cup water	
	Water	¼	cup flour	
4	slices bacon	¾	cup cider vinegar	
¼	cup chopped onion	3 to 4	tablespoons sugar	
2	tablespoon sliced green onions	1	teaspoon salt	
2	tablespoons chopped red or green pepper	⅛	teaspoon pepper	
1	rib celery, sliced	2	hard-cooked eggs, chopped	
		1	tablespoon minced parsley	

Arrange potatoes in skillet. Add 1 inch water; cook, covered, at 400° until boiling. Reduce heat to simmer, between Warm and 200°; cook, covered, until potatoes are fork-tender, 15 to 20 minutes. Drain potatoes; cool until warm and cut into ½-inch cubes. Reserve.

Cook bacon in skillet at 300° until crisp. Remove and crumble when cool. Pour off excess drippings, reserving 2 tablespoons in skillet. Add onions, red pepper, and celery; cook at 300° until onions are tender, about 3 minutes. Combine water and flour in small bowl. Stir into skillet with vinegar, sugar, salt, and pepper; cook until thickened, stirring constantly. Pour sauce over reserved potatoes, toss. Add bacon, eggs, and parsley; toss until blended. Refrigerate several hours for flavors to blend.

6 servings

Dilled Potato Nuggets

2	tablespoons vegetable oil	½	teaspoon dried dillweed	
1	tablespoon butter or margarine	¼	teaspoon onion powder	
4	cups frozen potato nuggets	¼	teaspoon paprika	

Heat oil and butter in skillet at Warm until butter is melted. Stir in potato nuggets; cook, covered, at 275° until browned and crisp, 5 to 6 minutes, stirring occasionally. Sprinkle potatoes with dillweed, onion powder, and paprika; cook 1 minute.

4 servings

Potatoes Gratin

2	pounds potatoes, peeled, cut into ½-inch cubes	2	cups half-and-half
	Salt and white pepper	1	tablespoon grated Parmesan cheese
			Nutmeg

Arrange potatoes in skillet; sprinkle lightly with salt and pepper. Pour half-and-half over potatoes; cook, covered, at 250° for 10 minutes, stirring frequently. Reduce heat to Warm; cook, covered, until potatoes are tender and half-and-half is almost absorbed, about 25 minutes, stirring every 10 minutes. Sprinkle potatoes with cheese and nutmeg.

6 to 8 servings

Country Beans

6	slices bacon	1	15-ounce can kidney beans, drained
1	medium onion, sliced	1	14½-ounce can diced tomatoes
1	medium green pepper, sliced	2	tablespoons dark molasses
1	10-ounce package frozen green beans	2	teaspoons Worcestershire sauce
1	10-ounce package frozen baby lima beans	2	teaspoons prepared mustard
		2 to 3	drops hot pepper sauce
			Salt and pepper

Cook bacon in skillet at 300° until crisp. Remove bacon and crumble when cool. Pour off excess drippings, reserving 1 tablespoon in skillet. Add onion and green pepper; cook at 225° until tender, about 5 minutes. Stir in beans; cook, covered, 3 minutes, stirring occasionally. Stir in tomatoes, molasses, Worcestershire, mustard, and hot pepper sauce; cook at 400° until boiling. Reduce heat to simmer, between Warm and 200°; cook, covered, until lima beans are tender, 15 to 20 minutes. Season to taste with salt and pepper.

6 servings

New England Bean Bake

¾	pound bacon	½	cup maple syrup or light molasses
2	cups chopped onions	½	cup packed light brown sugar
4	16-ounce cans Great Northern beans, drained	1	teaspoon dry mustard
3½	cups water	1	teaspoon salt

Cook bacon in skillet at 300° until crisp. Remove bacon and crumble when cool. Pour off excess drippings, reserving 3 tablespoons in skillet. Add onions; cook at 225° until tender, stirring occasionally. Stir in bacon and remaining ingredients; cook at 400° until boiling. Reduce heat to simmer, between Warm and 200°; cook, covered, until beans are golden and most of liquid is absorbed, about 1¾ hours, stirring occasionally.

10 to 12 servings

Fruit and Sausage Stuffing

½	pound sausage	1	egg, beaten
8	tablespoons butter or margarine, divided	2	tablespoons minced parsley
1	pound loaf firm whole wheat bread, cut into 1-inch cubes	1½ to 2	teaspoons dried sage leaves
2	cups sliced mushrooms	1	teaspoon dried thyme leaves
1	cup thinly sliced celery	1	teaspoon dried rosemary leaves
¾	cup chopped onion	½	teaspoon salt
1¾ to 2	cups chicken broth	¼	teaspoon pepper
		1	cup chopped mixed dried fruit

Cook sausage in skillet at 250° until browned, breaking into pieces with a fork. Remove sausage; reserve. Discard drippings.

Heat 3 tablespoons butter in skillet at Warm until melted. Add half the bread cubes; cook at 300° until golden, stirring occasionally. Remove to large bowl. Add 3 tablespoons butter to skillet; cook remaining bread cubes. Remove to bowl.

Add remaining 2 tablespoons butter, mushrooms, celery, and onion to skillet; cook at 250° until onion is tender, about 4 minutes. Add vegetable mixture to bread cubes. Whisk 1¾ cup chicken broth and egg in small bowl; stir into bread cube mixture. Mix in parsley, sage, thyme, rosemary, salt, pepper, and remaining broth if desired for consistency. Stir in reserved sausage and fruit. Spoon stuffing into skillet; cook, covered, at 200° until fruit is tender, 15 to 20 minutes, stirring occasionally. Serve hot.

8 to 10 servings

Pasta with Roasted Garlic Tomato Sauce

1 medium garlic bulb (15 to 20 cloves)	1 tablespoon balsamic vinegar
2 tablespoons olive oil	¼ cup chopped fresh basil
½ cup pitted chopped kalamata olives	Salt and pepper
6 cups coarsely chopped plum tomatoes (about 2 pounds)	1 14- to 16-ounce package cavatappi or rotini pasta, cooked, drained
	Grated Parmesan cheese

Break cloves apart from garlic bulb, leaving a layer of papery skin surrounding each clove. Heat skillet at 250°. Toss garlic and oil together in skillet until garlic is coated with oil. Cook until garlic is soft, but not brown, about 20 minutes for small cloves and 30 minutes for large, stirring frequently. Remove cloves using a slotted spoon; cool. Remove papery skin from roasted cloves. Chop cloves into a paste; reserve.

Heat skillet at 250°. Add olives; cook 1 minute, stirring frequently. Add tomatoes; cook at 300° until soft and thickened, about 10 minutes. Stir in balsamic vinegar and reserved roasted garlic paste. Cook 2 minutes, stirring constantly. Add basil, salt, and pepper to taste; cook 1 minute. Serve sauce over hot cooked pasta. Sprinkle with Parmesan cheese as desired.

4 to 6 servings

Mexican Rice and Corn Casserole

4 cups cooked rice	⅛ teaspoon ground cumin
1 10-ounce package frozen whole kernel corn, thawed	½ cup shredded Monterey Jack cheese
½ cup sour cream	½ cup shredded cheddar cheese

Combine rice and corn in skillet; cook, covered at 350° until heated, about 5 minutes. Reduce heat to Warm. Stir in sour cream, cumin, and sprinkle with cheeses; cook, covered, until cheese is melted, about 3 minutes.

8 servings

Fruit and Nut Rice

1	tablespoon butter or margarine	¾	cup water	
¼	cup chopped celery	½	teaspoon chicken flavor instant bouillon	
1	tablespoon golden raisins			
1	tablespoon slivered almonds	¾	cup enriched precooked rice	
⅛	teaspoon ground cinnamon	¼	cup mandarin orange segments, drained	
⅛	teaspoon salt			

Heat butter in skillet at Warm until melted. Add celery; cook at 225° for 2 minutes. Stir in raisins, almonds, cinnamon, and salt; cook 2 minutes. Remove celery mixture from skillet. Stir water and bouillon into skillet; heat at 400° until boiling. Stir in rice; turn heat to Off and let stand, covered, until liquid is absorbed, about 5 minutes. Stir in celery mixture and orange segments; cook at 200° until heated, about 2 minutes.

2 servings

Pecan Rice

½	cup pecan halves	½	teaspoon dried thyme leaves	
2	tablespoons butter or margarine	⅛	teaspoon ground mace	
1	cup thinly sliced celery	1	6¼-ounce package fast-cooking long grain and wild rice	
¼	cup finely chopped onion		Salt and pepper	
2	cups water			
2	teaspoons chicken flavor instant bouillon			

Heat skillet at 300°. Add pecans; heat until toasted, about 2 to 3 minutes. Remove and reserve.

Heat butter in skillet at Warm until melted. Add celery and onion; cook 2 minutes. Stir in water, bouillon, thyme, and mace; heat at 400° until boiling. Stir in rice; omit seasoning packet. Reduce heat to simmer, between Warm and 200°; cook, covered, until rice is tender and all liquid is absorbed, about 5 minutes. Stir in reserved pecans; season to taste with salt and pepper.

4 servings

CHAPTER SIX

Meats

There are many factors to juggle when choosing a meat dish to serve. Not only individual tastes, but also cooking time, cost, occasion, and number of diners. The recipes in this chapter will expertly utilize the electric skillet to solve most any obstacle.

The skillet is a beacon of hope when time is of essence. Superb meals like *Rib-Eye Steaks Stroganoff, Pork Chops with Red Cabbage and Apples, Szechwan Beef and Peanuts,* and *Orange Ham Kabobs* can be cooked in under an hour. Charm any casual gathering with the bold flavors of *Southwestern Pot Pie* or *Sweet and Spicy Pork Stir-Fry* for a quick and economical meal.

For a quaint dinner party, your guests will be indulged in the elegance of *Veal Scallops Parmesan* or *Steaks Wellington with Bordelaise Sauce,* and you will take satisfaction in knowing the ease of preparation.

The skillet will even rise to the occasion when serving eight to ten or more with saucy *Beer Glazed Ham,* spice-fragrant *Greek-Style Lamb Roast,* or *Roast Pork Loin with Sweet-Sour Fruit.*

And, for those times when life gets a little frazzled, take pleasure in the comforting taste and aroma of *Home-Style Pot Roast* or *Savory Cheese Meat Loaf.* Regardless of what your agenda dishes out, let these recipes help you manage life's many challenges with ease.

Sauerbraten

2	cups water	3	pounds blade or center cut	
1	cup white wine vinegar		chuck roast	
3	medium onions, sliced, divided	3	slices bacon	
2	tablespoons pickling spice	2	whole cloves	
2	bay leaves, divided	½	cup raisins	
12	juniper berries, lightly crushed (optional)	10	gingersnaps, crushed (optional)	

Combine water, vinegar, 2 sliced onions, pickling spice, 1 bay leaf, and juniper berries in skillet; cook at 400° until boiling. Turn heat to Off; cool to room temperature. Place beef in glass baking dish; pour cooled marinade over meat. Refrigerate, covered, 2 to 3 days, turning meat over twice each day.

Remove meat from marinade; strain marinade, reserving liquid. Dry meat well with paper toweling.

Cook bacon in skillet at 300° until crisp. Remove and crumble when cool; reserve. Pour off excess drippings, reserving 1 tablespoon in skillet. Add meat; cook, covered, at 350° until browned, about 5 minutes on each side. Remove meat. Add remaining onion; cook at 225° for 10 minutes, stirring occasionally. Add meat, reserved marinade liquid, cloves, and remaining bay leaf; cook at 400° until boiling. Reduce heat to simmer, between Warm and 200°; cook, covered, until meat is tender, 1 to 1½ hours. Stir in reserved bacon, raisins, and gingersnaps during last 30 minutes of cooking time.

Shopping Tip: Juniper berries can be purchased in specialty food stores or the spice department of large super-markets. There is no substitute. If not available, omit from recipe.

4 to 6 servings

Italian Pot Roast

3½	pounds blade or center cut chuck roast	1	6-ounce can tomato paste
½	teaspoon salt	¾	teaspoon dried basil leaves
½	teaspoon pepper	½	cup sliced celery
2	tablespoons olive oil	½	cup coarsely chopped carrot
1	14½-ounce can diced tomatoes	½	cup sliced mushrooms
1	cup dry red wine	8	small potatoes
		6	small onions

Sprinkle both sides of meat with salt and pepper. Heat skillet at 350°. Add oil and meat; cook until browned on both sides. Add tomatoes, wine, tomato paste, and basil; cook at 400° until boiling. Reduce heat to simmer, between Warm and 200°; cook, covered, until meat is fork-tender, about 1¾ to 2 hours. Add celery, carrot, mushrooms, potatoes, and onions during last 45 minutes of cooking time.

6 to 8 servings

Home-Style Pot Roast

4	tablespoons flour, divided
½	teaspoon dry mustard
½	teaspoon salt
¼	teaspoon pepper
3½	pounds blade or center cut chuck roast
2	tablespoons vegetable oil
1	cup beer
1	teaspoon beef flavor instant bouillon
8	small potatoes
6	carrots, cut crosswise into halves
4	small whole onions
¼	cup cold water or milk
	Salt and pepper

Combine 2 tablespoons flour, mustard, salt, and pepper in small bowl. Coat meat with seasoned flour. Heat skillet at 350°. Add oil and meat; cook until well browned on both sides. Add beer and bouillon; cook at 400° until boiling. Reduce heat to simmer, between Warm and 200°; cook, covered, for 1 hour. Peel strip from centers of potatoes. Add potatoes, carrots, and onions; cook, covered, until meat is fork-tender, about 1 hour.

Arrange meat and vegetables on serving platter; keep warm. Stir remaining 2 tablespoons flour and water into pan juices; cook at 250°, until thickened, about 2 minutes, stirring constantly. Season to taste with salt and pepper. Serve gravy over meat.

6 to 8 servings

Savory Chuck Roast

2	tablespoons vegetable oil
4	pounds blade or center cut chuck roast
¼	cup chopped onion
1	clove garlic, minced
¼	cup all-purpose flour
2	cups warm water
¼	cup sweet vermouth (optional)
1	teaspoon beef flavor instant bouillon
3	peppercorns
1	bay leaf
1	whole clove
2	tablespoons chopped red pepper
	Salt and pepper

Heat skillet at 350°. Add oil and beef; cook until browned, about 5 minutes on each side. Remove meat. Add onion and garlic; cook at 225° until onion is tender, about 2 minutes. Stir in flour; cook 1 minute. Stir in water, vermouth, bouillon, peppercorns, bay leaf, and clove; cook at 400° until boiling, scraping drippings from bottom of skillet with plastic or wooden utensil. Reduce heat to simmer, between Warm and 200°. Add meat; cook, covered, until meat is tender, about 2 hours, turning meat over twice during cooking. Remove meat to serving platter. Stir red pepper into sauce; season to taste with salt and pepper. Serve sauce over meat.

6 to 8 servings

Saucy Swiss Steaks

½	cup all-purpose flour		½	cup chopped celery
½	teaspoon salt		1	15-ounce can tomato sauce
¼	teaspoon pepper		½	cup hot water
1¾	pounds round steak, cut into serving pieces		¼	teaspoon beef flavor instant bouillon
2	tablespoons vegetable oil		1	bay leaf
½	cup chopped onion		½	teaspoon dried basil leaves
1	clove garlic, minced			Salt and pepper
1	cup chopped green pepper			

Combine flour, salt, and pepper in small bowl. Coat meat with seasoned flour. Heat skillet at 350°. Add oil and meat; cook until well browned, about 5 minutes on each side. Remove meat.

Add onion and garlic; cook at 225° for 2 minutes. Stir in green pepper and celery; cook for 2 minutes. Stir in tomato sauce, water, bouillon, bay leaf, and basil; cook at 400° until boiling. Reduce heat to simmer, between Warm and 200°. Season to taste with salt and pepper. Return meat to skillet; cook, covered, until tender, 1½ to 1¾ hours.

4 to 6 servings

Country Fried Steak

1	pound round steak, excess fat trimmed, pounded to ¼-inch thickness		¼	cup vegetable oil
			1	large onion, sliced
¼	cup all-purpose flour		⅔	cup water
2	tablespoons dry bread crumbs		½	teaspoon beef flavor instant bouillon
½	teaspoon salt		2	tablespoons flour
¼	teaspoon paprika		⅔	cup milk
¼	teaspoon garlic powder			Salt and pepper
⅛	teaspoon pepper			

Cut round steak into 4 serving pieces. Combine ¼ cup flour, bread crumbs, salt, paprika, and garlic powder in small bowl. Coat meat with seasoned flour. Heat skillet at 350°. Add oil and steak; cook until well browned, about 2 minutes on each side. Remove steaks. Add onion; cook, covered, at 225°, until tender, about 5 minutes, stirring occasionally. Remove onion.

Stir in water and bouillon, scraping drippings from bottom of skillet with plastic or wooden utensil. Mix 2 tablespoons flour and milk in small bowl. Stir mixture into skillet; cook at 400° until mixture boils and thickens, stirring constantly. Add meat and onion, coating with gravy; cook at Warm, covered, until heated through, about 5 minutes.

4 servings

Mexican Flank Steak with Salsa

1½ pounds flank steak, excess fat trimmed	¼ teaspoon dried marjoram leaves
1 cup tomato juice	⅛ teaspoon ground cumin
2 tablespoons distilled white vinegar	⅛ teaspoon pepper
1 tablespoon sugar	**Mexican Salsa** (see recipe below)
1 teaspoon Worcestershire sauce	2 tablespoons vegetable oil

Pound flank steak until ¾ inch thick. Score steak diagonally in diamond pattern on both sides, using sharp knife. Place steak in shallow glass baking dish. Mix tomato juice, vinegar, sugar, Worcestershire, marjoram, cumin, and pepper in small bowl; pour over steak. Refrigerate 4 to 6 hours, turning steak occasionally.

Make Mexican Salsa; remove from skillet and refrigerate.

Remove steak from marinade; reserve marinade. Heat skillet at 350°. Add oil and steak; cook until browned on both sides. Add reserved marinade; heat at 400° until boiling. Reduce heat to simmer, between Warm and 200°; cook, covered, 30 minutes. Stir in Mexican Salsa; cook, covered, until steak is tender, about 30 minutes.

6 servings

Mexican Salsa

1 tablespoon vegetable oil	2 tablespoons cider vinegar
½ cup chopped onion	2 teaspoons sugar
1 clove garlic, minced	½ teaspoon dried coriander leaves
2 14½-ounce cans diced tomatoes	½ teaspoon salt
1 4-ounce can chopped green chiles	

Heat skillet at 250°. Add oil, onion, and garlic; cook until tender, 2 to 3 minutes. Stir in remaining ingredients; cook at 400° until boiling. Reduce heat to simmer, between Warm and 200°; cook until slightly thickened, 8 to 10 minutes.

Preparation Tip: Mexican Salsa can be made in advance. Refrigerate, covered, up to 2 weeks.

About 1¼ cups

Italian Beef on Noodles

¾	cup beef broth	¼	teaspoon dried marjoram leaves
3	tablespoons olive oil, divided	1	clove garlic, minced
3	tablespoons red wine vinegar	¾	pound flank or round steak, thinly sliced
1	tablespoon Worcestershire sauce		
1	tablespoon cornstarch	1	medium onion, sliced
2	teaspoons sugar	1	large green pepper, sliced
1	teaspoon crushed red pepper		Hot buttered egg noodles
¼	teaspoon dried basil leaves		

Mix beef broth, 1 tablespoon oil, vinegar, Worcestershire, cornstarch, sugar, red pepper, basil, marjoram, and garlic in shallow glass baking dish; add beef, stirring to coat pieces evenly. Refrigerate, covered, 2 to 3 hours, stirring occasionally.

Remove beef from marinade; reserve marinade. Heat skillet at 225°. Add remaining 2 tablespoons oil, onion, and green pepper; cook until tender, 3 to 4 minutes, stirring constantly. Stir in beef; cook at 350° until beef is brown, about 3 minutes, stirring constantly. Stir in reserved marinade; cook until thickened, 1 to 2 minutes, stirring frequently. Serve beef mixture over noodles.

4 servings

Szechwan Beef and Peanuts

1	egg white, beaten	1 to 1½	teaspoons minced fresh gingerroot
1	tablespoon dry sherry		
1	tablespoon soy sauce	¼ to ½	teaspoon crushed red pepper
1	tablespoon cornstarch	½	cup water
½	teaspoon sesame oil (optional)	¼	teaspoon beef flavor instant bouillon
1	pound flank steak, cut across the grain into ⅛-inch slices		
		3	green onions, cut into 2-inch pieces
2	tablespoons peanut oil	⅓	cup unsalted cocktail peanuts
1	clove garlic, minced		Hot cooked rice

Mix egg white, sherry, soy sauce, cornstarch, and sesame oil in small bowl; pour over steak in shallow glass baking dish, stirring to coat pieces evenly. Let stand 30 minutes.

Heat skillet at 225°. Add oil, garlic, gingerroot, and red pepper; cook 1 minute. Remove beef from marinade; reserve marinade. Add beef; stir-fry at 350° until beef is brown, about 2 minutes. Stir in water, bouillon, and reserved marinade; cook until thickened, about 1 minute. Cut onion pieces lengthwise into fourths. Stir onions and peanuts into beef mixture; cook 1 minute. Serve over rice.

4 servings

Steaks Wellington with Bordelaise Sauce

1	sheet frozen puff pastry, thawed	1	bay leaf
1	tablespoon butter or margarine	2	whole peppercorns
1	tablespoon vegetable oil	1	cup water
4	beef tenderloin or rib eye steaks, ¾ inch thick	1	teaspoon beef flavor instant bouillon
	Salt and pepper	1	tablespoon cornstarch
2	tablespoons minced onion	2	tablespoons cold water
½	cup red wine	2	ounces liver pâté or high quality liverwurst
¼	teaspoon dried thyme leaves		

Cut 4 rounds from puff pastry using cutter approximately 1 inch smaller in diameter than the steaks. Cut piece of parchment to fit rack; place on rack in skillet. Heat skillet at 350°. Place pastry rounds on paper; bake, covered, until puffed and crisp, about 25 minutes. Remove and cool pastry rounds.

Heat butter and oil in skillet at Warm until butter is melted. Lightly sprinkle steaks with salt and pepper. Place in skillet; cook at 350° to desired degree of doneness, 3 minutes on each side for medium. Remove from skillet; keep warm. Reserve pan drippings.

Reduce heat to 225°. Add onion to reserved drippings; cook 1 minute. Stir in wine, thyme, bay leaf, and peppercorns; cook 3 minutes, stirring frequently. Stir in water and bouillon, scraping drippings from bottom of skillet with plastic or wooden utensil. Heat at 400° until boiling. Mix cornstarch and cold water in small bowl. Stir into sauce; cook until thickened, stirring constantly. Strain, discard herbs.

Place steaks on serving plates. Cut pâté into 4 slices; place on steaks. Spoon sauce over; top with reserved pastry rounds.

4 servings

Rib-Eye Steaks Stroganoff

2	tablespoons vegetable oil		¼	teaspoon dried thyme leaves
4	rib eye steaks, ¾ inch thick		¼	teaspoon salt
	Salt and pepper		⅛	teaspoon pepper
3	cups sliced mushrooms		⅓	cup half-and-half
¾	cup chopped red or green pepper		3	tablespoons cream cheese, softened
½	teaspoon dried marjoram leaves			

Heat oil in skillet at 350°. Add steaks; cook to desired degree of doneness, about 3 minutes on each side for medium. Sprinkle lightly with salt and pepper; remove to serving platter; keep warm.

Add mushrooms and red pepper to skillet; cook at 225° for 2 minutes, scraping drippings from bottom of skillet with plastic or wooden utensil. Stir in marjoram, thyme, salt, and pepper; cook 2 minutes. Mix half-and-half and cream cheese until smooth in small bowl. Add to skillet; cook until heated through, stirring constantly. Spoon vegetable mixture over steaks and serve immediately.

Substitution Tip: Any tender beef steaks may be used in place of rib eye steaks.

4 servings

Mushroom Salisbury Steaks

1	pound lean ground beef		⅛	teaspoon pepper
1	tablespoon tomato paste		1½	cups beef broth
1	tablespoon dried chives		2	cups sliced mushrooms
½	teaspoon salt		1½	tablespoons cornstarch
¼	teaspoon ground nutmeg, divided		⅓	cup dry white wine or water

Mix ground beef, tomato paste, chives, salt, ⅛ teaspoon nutmeg, and pepper in medium bowl; form mixture into 4 oval patties. Heat skillet at 350°. Add beef patties; cook until thermometer inserted into patties registers 160°, about 5 to 7 minutes, turning patties occasionally. Remove patties; pour excess drippings from skillet.

Add beef broth to skillet and heat at 400° until boiling. Reduce heat to simmer, between Warm and 200°. Add mushrooms; cook 3 minutes, stirring occasionally. Mix cornstarch and wine in small bowl; stir into broth mixture until thickened. Stir in remaining ⅛ teaspoon nutmeg. Add beef patties; cook, covered, until heated through, about 2 minutes.

4 servings

Acapulco Tostadas

Mexican Beef (see recipe below)
1 cup refried beans
2 cups shredded lettuce
1 medium tomato, chopped
1 avocado, peeled, pitted, chopped
¼ cup sliced black olives

2 green onions, sliced
8 flat tostadas (5¼-inch diameter)
Salsa
Shredded cheddar cheese
Sour cream

Make Mexican Beef; remove from skillet and keep warm.

Reduce heat to 250°. Add refried beans to skillet, stirring pan juice into beans. Cook, until heated through, about 2 minutes. Remove and reserve.

Combine lettuce, tomato, avocado, olives, and onions in medium bowl. Spread 2 tablespoons refried beans on each tostada. Spoon Mexican Beef evenly over beans, dividing equally between tostadas. Divide lettuce mixture equally between tostadas. Top each tostada with salsa, cheese, and sour cream, as desired.

Shopping Tip: Tostadas can be found in the ethnic section of the supermarket or in a Hispanic market.

8 servings

Mexican Beef

1 pound lean ground beef
½ cup chopped onion
1 clove garlic, minced
1 10-ounce can mild
   enchilada sauce

2 teaspoons chili powder
¼ teaspoon salt
¼ teaspoon cumin

Heat skillet at 350°. Add ground beef, onion, and garlic; cook until beef is brown, about 5 minutes, stirring occasionally. Pour off excess drippings. Stir in chili powder, salt, and cumin; cook until thickened, about 5 minutes.

About 2 cups

Southwestern Pot Pie

2	pounds lean ground beef	¼	teaspoon salt
¾	cup chopped onion	¼	teaspoon pepper
1	clove garlic	2	8½-ounce packages corn muffin mix
1	cup mild or hot chile salsa	2	eggs
⅓	cup sliced black olives	⅔	cup milk
½	teaspoon dried oregano leaves	2 to 3	teaspoons chili powder
¼	teaspoon ground cumin	1	cup shredded cheddar cheese

Heat skillet at 350°. Add beef, onion, and garlic; cook until beef is browned, stirring occasionally. Pour off excess drippings. Stir in salsa, olives, oregano, cumin, salt, and pepper; cook, covered, at 200° for 5 minutes.

Make corn muffin mix according to package directions, using eggs, milk, and chili powder; fold in cheese. Spoon batter over beef mixture in skillet; cook at 225°, with cover 1 inch ajar, until batter is cooked through, about 20 to 25 minutes.

8 servings

Swedish Meatballs

1	pound ground beef	⅛	teaspoon pepper
½	pound ground pork	⅛	teaspoon ground nutmeg
½	cup milk	⅛	teaspoon ground ginger
¼	cup minced onion	2	tablespoons vegetable oil
1	egg, beaten	2	tablespoons all-purpose flour
1	cup soft bread crumbs	1½	cups hot beef broth
1	tablespoon dried parsley	2	tablespoons sour cream
1	teaspoon salt		

Combine meats, milk, onion, egg, bread crumbs, parsley, salt, pepper, nutmeg, and ginger in medium bowl. Mix by hand until well combined; chill for 1 to 2 hours.

Shape meat mixture into ½-inch balls. Heat skillet at 350°. Add meatballs; cook until browned on all sides. Remove meatballs. Reduce heat to 275°. Add oil to drippings in skillet. Stir in flour until bubbly. Add broth; cook until thickened, stirring constantly. Return meatballs to skillet; heat, covered, until cooked through, about 10 to 12 minutes. Stir in sour cream and heat through.

4 servings

Savory Cheese Meat Loaf

1 pound lean ground beef	½ cup uncooked oats
1 pound ground pork	⅓ cup chopped green pepper
1 cup shredded cheddar cheese, divided	¼ cup chopped onion
1 3-ounce package cream cheese, softened	2 tablespoons milk
2 eggs	2 tablespoons Worcestershire sauce
½ cup ketchup, divided	½ teaspoon salt
	¼ teaspoon pepper

Mix all ingredients, except ¼ cup cheddar cheese and ¼ cup ketchup in medium bowl; form into round or oval loaf in skillet. Spread remaining ¼ cup ketchup on top; cook, covered, at 200° until a thermometer inserted into the meat loaf registers 160°, about 55 to 60 minutes. Sprinkle top of loaf with remaining ¼ cup cheese; cook, covered, until cheese is melted, about 3 minutes. Remove to serving platter; let stand 10 minutes before slicing.

8 servings

Beer-Steamed Brats

1 12-ounce can beer	8 brat or hot dog buns
1 teaspoon beef flavor instant bouillon	3 tablespoons mayonnaise
1 teaspoon dried rosemary leaves	3 tablespoons Bavarian-style mustard
8 fully cooked bratwursts or other sausages	3 tablespoons finely chopped dill pickle
	1 teaspoon prepared horseradish

Heat beer, bouillon, and rosemary in skillet at 400° until boiling. Reduce heat to simmer, between Warm and 200°. Arrange bratwursts on rack in skillet; cook, covered, until heated through, 10 to 15 minutes. Wrap buns loosely in aluminum foil; place on rack in skillet during last 5 minutes of cooking time.

Mix mayonnaise, mustard, pickle, and horseradish in small bowl. Place bratwursts in buns; serve with mayonnaise mixture.

8 servings

Sausage and Cheese Manicotti with White Sauce

Parmesan White Sauce
(see recipe below)

½ pound mild or hot Italian sausage, casing removed, crumbled

½ cup finely chopped onion

1 clove garlic, minced

2 cups ricotta cheese

2 eggs, beaten

½ 10-ounce package frozen spinach, thawed and squeezed dry

2 tablespoons grated Parmesan cheese

½ teaspoon salt

⅛ teaspoon pepper

⅛ teaspoon ground cinnamon

8 manicotti shells, cooked

2 cups spaghetti sauce

1 cup shredded mozzarella cheese

Make Parmesan White Sauce; remove to bowl. Clean skillet.

Cook sausage in skillet at 325° until brown. Add onion and garlic; cook at 225° for 5 minutes. Remove sausage from skillet and drain.

Mix ricotta cheese and eggs in medium bowl. Stir spinach into ricotta cheese mixture. Stir in sausage, Parmesan, salt, pepper, and cinnamon; stuff mixture into manicotti shells.

Spread spaghetti sauce in bottom of skillet; arrange stuffed manicotti over sauce. Spoon Parmesan White Sauce over manicotti. Sprinkle with mozzarella cheese; cook, covered, at 200° until manicotti are heated through, about 30 minutes.

4 servings

Parmesan White Sauce

¼ cup butter or margarine

¼ cup all-purpose flour

2 cups milk

1 cup half-and-half

¼ cup grated Parmesan cheese

½ teaspoon grated lemon peel

½ teaspoon salt

⅛ teaspoon white pepper

⅛ teaspoon ground nutmeg

Heat butter in skillet at Warm until melted. Stir in flour, cook 1 minute. Stir in milk and half-and-half; cook at 400° until boiling. Reduce heat to simmer, between Warm and 200°; cook until sauce is thickened, stirring constantly. Turn heat to Off; stir in remaining ingredients.

About 3 cups

Saucy Barbecued Spareribs

Hot Chili Barbecue Sauce
(see recipe below)
4 pounds pork spareribs, cut into
   serving pieces

4 cups water
1 cup cider vinegar

Make Hot Chili Barbecue Sauce; remove to bowl. Clean skillet.

Arrange ribs in skillet, meat sides down. Add water and vinegar; heat at 400° until boiling. Reduce heat to simmer, between Warm and 200°; cook, with cover ½ inch ajar, for 30 minutes or until pork is tender. Remove meat; pour off liquid.

Replace meat in skillet and pour Hot Chili Barbecue Sauce over ribs; cook, covered, at Warm for 10 minutes. Turn ribs over; cook, covered, 10 minutes. Uncover and cook at 200° for 2 minutes on each side.

Substitution Tip: Any desired barbecue sauce may be substituted for the Hot Chili Barbecue Sauce.

4 servings

Hot Chili Barbecue Sauce

2 10-ounce jars apricot preserves
1 cup chili sauce
2 tablespoons distilled white
   vinegar
1 tablespoon Worcestershire sauce

3 to 3½ tablespoons chili powder
1 clove garlic, minced
¼ teaspoon ground ginger
4 to 6 drops hot pepper sauce

Mix all ingredients in skillet; cook at 400° until boiling. Reduce heat to simmer, between Warm and 200°; cook 10 minutes.

Preparation Tip: Hot Chili Barbecue Sauce can be made in advance. Refrigerate, covered, up to 1 month.

About 3 cups

Pork Cutlets with Onion and Fennel

1 tablespoon vegetable oil
2 pork cutlets or chops, ¾ inch thick
¼ cup chopped onion
1 cup water

½ teaspoon chicken flavor instant
   bouillon
⅛ teaspoon fennel seed, crushed
⅛ teaspoon white pepper

Heat skillet at 350°. Add oil and pork cutlets; cook, covered, until brown, about 2 minutes on each side. Remove pork cutlets. Add onion; cook at 225° for 1 minute. Stir in remaining ingredients; cook at 400° until boiling. Reduce heat to simmer; between Warm and 200°. Add pork cutlets; cook, covered, until cutlets are tender, about 15 to 20 minutes.

2 servings

Stuffed Pork Chops

2	tablespoons vegetable oil, divided		1⅔	cups water
½	cup chopped green pepper		¼	cup butter or margarine
¼	cup chopped onion		6	pork chops, 1 inch thick
½	cup whole kernel corn			Salt and pepper
1	6-ounce package stuffing mix for pork		¾	cup water
			½	teaspoon chicken flavor instant bouillon

Heat 1 tablespoon oil in skillet at 225°. Add green pepper and onion; cook until tender, about 5 minutes. Stir in corn. Remove vegetable mixture from skillet. Clean skillet.

Make stuffing mix in skillet according to package directions, using 1⅔ cups water and ¼ cup butter; cook at 200° for 4 minutes. Stir in vegetable mixture. Cut pockets in pork chops; spoon stuffing into each chop. Wrap remaining stuffing in aluminum foil; reserve. Clean skillet.

Heat remaining 1 tablespoon oil in skillet at 325°. Add pork chops; cook until browned, about 4 minutes on each side. Pour off excess drippings. Sprinkle chops lightly with salt and pepper. Add ¾ cup water and bouillon; heat at 400° until boiling. Reduce heat to simmer, between Warm and 200°; cook, covered, until pork chops are tender, 45 minutes to 1 hour; turning after 20 minutes. Add more water, if necessary. Add reserved foil package of stuffing to skillet during last 20 minutes of cooking time.

4 to 6 servings

Pork Chops with Red Cabbage and Apples

4	boneless center loin pork chops, ¾ inch thick		¼	cup firmly packed brown sugar
4	slices bacon		¼	cup water
4	cups sliced red cabbage		2	tablespoons balsamic vinegar
2	cups cored chopped red cooking apples (Braeburn, Gala, Jonagold)		2	tablespoons country-style Dijon mustard
1	cup thinly sliced red onion		1	teaspoon caraway seeds

Preheat skillet at 325°. Add pork chops; cook until browned, 1 to 2 minutes per side. Remove from skillet; keep warm.

Cook bacon in skillet at 300°. Remove bacon and crumble when cool; reserve.

Pour off excess drippings, reserving 1 tablespoon in skillet. Add cabbage, apples, and onion; cook for 3 minutes. Stir in brown sugar, water, vinegar, mustard, and caraway seed until well blended. Add browned pork chops, making sure some of vegetable mixture covers each. Cook at 250°, covered, until cabbage is tender, about 15 to 20 minutes. Stir in reserved bacon.

4 servings

Sweet and Spicy Pork Stir-Fry

3	tablespoons soy sauce	1	8-ounce can pineapple chunks, drained, juice reserved	
1	tablespoon water	2	tablespoons vegetable oil	
2	cloves garlic, minced	1	large green bell pepper, sliced	
1	teaspoon grated gingerroot	¼	teaspoon crushed red pepper	
1	teaspoon sugar		Hot cooked rice	
1	pound diced pork			
2	teaspoons cornstarch			

Mix soy sauce, water, garlic, gingerroot, and sugar in medium bowl; pour over pork in shallow glass baking dish. Refrigerate for 30 minutes to 1 hour, stirring occasionally.

Mix cornstarch and reserved pineapple juice in small bowl. Set aside.

Heat oil in skillet at 375°. Add pork and marinade. Stir-fry for 2 to 3 minutes until pork is brown but not quite done. Add bell pepper; cook, covered, at 250° until peppers are crisp-tender, about 2 minutes. Pour reserved pineapple juice mixture into skillet, stirring well before adding. Stir in pineapple chunks and red pepper. Cook and stir until thickened and clear, about 1 to 2 minutes. Serve over rice.

4 servings

Cinnamon Fruit Pork Roast

1	7-ounce package mixed dried fruit, coarsely chopped	1	small bay leaf	
1	cup apricot nectar	1	cardamom pod, lightly crushed	
¼	cup almond flavor liqueur or peach nectar	⅛	teaspoon ground nutmeg	
1	cinnamon stick	2½	pounds boneless rolled pork loin roast Salt and pepper	
1	whole clove	1	tablespoon vegetable oil	
		1	cup water	

Place fruit, apricot nectar, liqueur, cinnamon, clove, bay leaf, cardamom, and nutmeg in skillet; cook at 400° until boiling. Reduce heat to simmer, between Warm and 200°; cook, covered, 20 minutes. Remove fruit mixture, cool. Discard cinnamon stick, clove, and bay leaf. Clean skillet.

Unroll roast; sprinkle lightly with salt and pepper. Spread fruit mixture on roast reserving any excess for garnish; roll up and tie. Heat skillet at 350°. Add oil and roast; cook until browned on all sides, about 10 minutes. Remove roast. Add water to skillet; heat at 400° until boiling. Reduce heat to simmer, between Warm and 200°. Insert meat thermometer in roast, with tip of thermometer in center of meat, away from fat. Place roast on rack in skillet; cook, covered, until thermometer inserted in roast registers 155° for medium, about 2 hours. Remove roast to serving platter; let stand 15 minutes before slicing.

6 to 8 servings

Roast Pork Loin with Sweet-Sour Fruit

5	pounds pork loin roast	1	10-ounce can Mandarin orange segments, drained, juice reserved
1	tablespoon soy sauce	½	cup water
1	cup water	½	teaspoon chicken flavor instant bouillon
1	tablespoon vegetable oil	¼	cup cider vinegar
1	medium green pepper, cut into strips	3	tablespoons soy sauce
1	medium red pepper, cut into chunks	3	tablespoons tomato sauce
3	green onions, sliced diagonally	2	tablespoons cornstarch
1	clove garlic, minced	1	tablespoon sugar
1	20-ounce can sliced pineapple, drained, juice reserved	⅛	teaspoon ground ginger

Place roast on rack in skillet; brush with 1 tablespoon soy sauce. Insert meat thermometer in roast, with tip of thermometer in center of meat, away from fat and bone. Add 1 cup water to skillet; cook at 400° until boiling. Reduce heat to simmer, between Warm and 200°; cook, covered, until thermometer inserted into roast registers 155° for medium, about 2¾ to 3 hours. Remove roast to serving platter; let stand 15 minutes before slicing, loosely covered with aluminum foil. Clean skillet.

Heat skillet at 250°. Add oil, peppers, onions, and garlic; cook until peppers are crisp-tender, about 3 minutes. Mix reserved fruit juices and remaining ingredients, except fruit. Stir into pepper mixture; cook, until thickened, stirring constantly. Add pineapple slices and orange segments; cook until heated through, about 3 minutes. Serve fruit mixture with roast.

8 servings

Beer-Glazed Ham

5	pounds fully cooked boneless ham Whole cloves	3	tablespoons spicy brown mustard
		1	12-ounce can beer or ginger ale, divided
¾	cup packed light brown sugar	2 to 3	cups water

Score fat on top of ham; stud with cloves. Place ham on rack in skillet; insert meat thermometer in ham, with tip of thermometer in center of meat, away from fat.

Mix brown sugar, mustard, and 2 tablespoons beer in small bowl; spoon mixture over ham. Add remaining beer and 2 cups water to skillet; heat at 400° until boiling. Reduce heat to simmer, between Warm and 200°; cook, covered, until thermometer inserted in ham registers 135°, about 1½ hours. Baste ham with pan juices every 15 minutes; add remaining water if juices become too thick. Remove ham to serving platter; baste with pan juices. Let stand 10 minutes before slicing, loosely covered with aluminum foil.

12 to 14 servings

Orange Ham Kabobs

¼ cup orange marmalade
1 tablespoon soy sauce
1 teaspoon Dijon-style mustard
⅛ teaspoon ground ginger
8 ounces baked ham, cut into
  1-inch cubes

1 medium orange, cut into
  8 wedges
8 medium mushrooms
  Vegetable oil

Mix orange marmalade, soy sauce, mustard, and ginger in small bowl. Reserve.

Arrange ham, orange wedges, and mushrooms alternately on 4 metal skewers. Heat skillet at 300°. Brush bottom of skillet lightly with oil. Arrange skewers in skillet; cook until light brown, about 2 minutes on each side. Brush reserved marmalade mixture generously on kabobs; cook for 3 to 4 minutes, brushing several times with marmalade mixture.

2 servings

Greek Shish Kabobs

1½ pounds lean boneless lamb or
  beef, cut into 1-inch cubes
24 mushrooms
2 medium zucchini, cut into
  ½-inch pieces
2 medium onions, cut into wedges
¼ cup white wine vinegar
2 tablespoons olive oil

½ teaspoon sugar
1 clove garlic, minced
½ teaspoon dried oregano leaves
½ teaspoon dried mint leaves
½ teaspoon salt
¼ teaspoon pepper
  Hot cooked rice

Combine lamb, mushrooms, zucchini, and onions in shallow glass baking dish. Mix vinegar, oil, sugar, garlic, oregano, mint, salt, and pepper in small bowl; pour over meat and vegetables. Refrigerate, covered, 4 to 6 hours, stirring occasionally.

Remove lamb and vegetables from marinade; discard marinade. Arrange meat and vegetables alternately on 12 metal skewers. Heat skillet at 300°. Arrange skewers in skillet; cook until meat is browned and cooked to desired degree of doneness, 2 to 3 minutes on each side for medium. Serve with rice.

6 servings

Greek-Style Lamb Roast

2	tablespoons butter or margarine		5	cups water
1	cup pine nuts or slivered almonds		2	teaspoons chicken flavor instant bouillon
½	cup finely chopped onion			Salt and pepper
2	cloves garlic, minced		4	pounds boneless rolled leg of lamb
2	cups white long grain rice		2	large cloves garlic, cut into slivers
2	teaspoons ground cinnamon		1	teaspoon dried mint leaves
½	teaspoon ground allspice		1	egg, beaten
¼	teaspoon ground nutmeg		2	tablespoons olive oil
¼	teaspoon ground cloves		2	cups water
1	small bay leaf			

Heat butter in skillet at Warm until melted. Add pine nuts; cook at 225° until golden. Remove pine nuts; reserve. Add onion and minced garlic; cook 1 minute. Add rice, cinnamon, allspice, nutmeg, cloves, and bay leaf; cook 1 minute, stirring constantly. Stir in 5 cups water and bouillon; heat at 400° until boiling. Reduce heat to simmer, between Warm and 200°; cook, covered, until rice is tender and water absorbed, about 20 minutes. Remove bay leaf. Stir reserved pine nuts into rice mixture; season to taste with salt and pepper. Remove rice mixture. Clean skillet.

Unroll lamb. Make small incisions in meat; insert garlic slivers. Sprinkle meat lightly with mint, salt, and pepper. Mix 1½ cups of rice mixture with egg; spoon onto meat, leaving 1½-inch margin around edges of meat. Roll up and tie.

Heat skillet at 350°. Add oil; cook roast until browned on all sides. Remove roast. Insert meat thermometer so that tip is in center of meat, away from fat. Place meat on rack in skillet. Add 2 cups water; heat at 400° until boiling. Reduce heat to simmer, between Warm and 200°; cook, covered, until thermometer in roast registers 155°, about 1 hour.

Spoon remaining rice mixture into small covered heat-proof casserole or dish; place on rack with meat during last 20 minutes of cooking time. Remove roast to serving platter, let stand 15 minutes before slicing, loosely covered with aluminum foil. Serve rice with roast.

10 to 12 servings

Lamb Chops with Mint Sauce

6 lamb loin or rib chops, ¾ inch thick
Salt and pepper
2 tablespoons vegetable oil
¼ cup water

¼ cup mint jelly
¼ cup peach preserves
½ teaspoon dried mint leaves

Heat skillet at 350°. Sprinkle chops lightly with salt and pepper. Add oil and chops; cook until browned and no longer pink in the center, about 3 minutes on each side. Remove chops; keep warm. Discard fat.

Reduce temperature to 200°; add water to skillet, scraping drippings from bottom of skillet with plastic or wooden utensil. Add jelly, preserves, and mint; cook until jelly and preserves are melted, stirring constantly. Serve sauce with lamb.

4 to 6 servings

Veal Scallops Parmesan

1 pound veal scallops or cutlets
¼ cup all-purpose flour
Salt and pepper
¼ cup dry bread crumbs
2 tablespoons grated Parmesan cheese
1 teaspoon dried basil leaves, divided
½ teaspoon dried oregano leaves, divided

½ teaspoon salt
¼ teaspoon pepper
2 eggs, beaten
2 tablespoons olive oil
1 14½-ounce can diced Italian plum tomatoes, drained
1 cup tomato sauce
1 clove garlic, minced
½ teaspoon sugar
2 cups shredded mozzarella cheese

Pound veal until ¼ inch thick; cut into serving pieces. Mix flour, salt, and pepper in small bowl; reserve. Mix bread crumbs, Parmesan, ¼ teaspoon basil, ¼ teaspoon oregano, salt, and pepper in small bowl. Coat veal pieces lightly with flour mixture; dip into beaten egg; coat generously with crumb mixture.

Heat skillet at 350°. Add oil and veal; cook until golden, about 1 to 2 minutes on each side. Remove veal from skillet; drain on paper toweling. Discard excess drippings from skillet. Return veal to skillet. Combine tomatoes, tomato sauce, garlic, sugar, remaining 1 teaspoon basil, and remaining ¼ teaspoon oregano in medium bowl; pour over veal and sprinkle with cheese. Cook, covered, until cheese melts, about 5 minutes.

4 to 6 servings

Veal Marsala

1½	pounds veal scallops		2	tablespoons olive oil
½	cup all-purpose flour		⅔	cup Marsala wine
¼	teaspoon salt		2	tablespoons butter or margarine
⅛	teaspoon white pepper		1	teaspoon dried chives

Pound veal until ⅛ inch thick; cut into serving pieces. Combine flour, salt, and pepper in small bowl. Coat veal lightly with seasoned flour. Heat skillet at 350°. Add oil and veal; cook until browned, about 1 minute on each side. Remove veal.

Stir wine into skillet, scraping drippings from bottom of skillet with plastic or wooden utensil. Stir in butter, stir until thickened, about 3 minutes. Stir in chives. Return veal to skillet; cook at Warm until heated, turning to coat with sauce. Serve sauce with veal.

6 to 8 serving

Osso Bucco

4	pounds veal shanks (6 pieces)		1	28-ounce can diced Italian plum tomatoes
	Flour			
2	tablespoons olive oil		⅓	cup dry white wine or chicken broth
2	medium carrots, finely chopped		1	teaspoon grated lemon peel
2	ribs celery, thinly sliced		½	teaspoon dried basil leaves
1	medium red onion, chopped			Salt and pepper
1	clove garlic, minced			Hot cooked rice

Coat veal shanks lightly with flour. Heat skillet at 350°. Add oil and veal; cook until browned on all sides, about 10 minutes. Stir in carrots, celery, onion, and garlic; cook until tender, 3 to 5 minutes, stirring frequently. Add tomatoes, wine, lemon peel, and basil; cook at 400° until boiling. Reduce heat to simmer, between Warm and 200°; cook, covered, until tender, 1½ to 2 hours. Season to taste with salt and pepper. Serve with rice.

6 servings

Almond Cream Cheese
Coffee Cake, page 24

Mexican Breakfast
Wraps, page 13

Pork and Kraut Casserole, page 126
Stuffed Pork Chops, page 68

76

Fresh Strawberry Tart, page 145
Chocolate Fudge Cheesecake, page 152
Pears Poached in Port Wine, page 142

Asian Chicken and Vegetable
Stir-Fry, page 102

Saucy Barbecued Spareribs,
page 67

79

Shrimp Rolls, page 137
Greek-Style Pitas, page 140

Deep-Pan Pizza, page 125

Stirred Vanilla Custard, page 143
Fruit and Nut Filled Apples, page 142
Sour Cream Rhubarb Cake, page 147

Steamed Trout with Red Pepper
Sauce, page 109

Mushroom Salisbury Steaks, page 62

Lemon Chicken, page 104

83

Summer Vegetable Frittata, page 43
Silky Apricot Crêpes, page 23

Spice-Rubbed Tuna with Fruit Salsa, page 113
Sautéed Balsamic Tomatoes, page 38

Saucy Swiss Steaks, page 58

Savory Chuck Roast, page 57

Orange Chicken with Raisins
and Almonds, page 100

87

Mexican Flank Steak with Salsa, page 59
Sugared Cookies, page 149

Chicken and Shrimp
Paella, page 96

Sweet and Spicy
Pork Stir-Fry,
page 69

89

Jalapeño Corn Cakes, page 39

Chicken Tostadas with
Chipotle Salsa, page 95

Poultry

Years ago, "a chicken in every pot" meant prosperity and a meal on the table. In today's world, time and health are the primary focus and "boneless skinless chicken breasts in every freezer" translates to a quick and healthy meal on demand. Whether boneless skinless chicken breasts, a whole chicken, or turkey, poultry is the mainstay of American meals. It's low in calories, cooks quickly, and tastes great…even to finicky children. Best of all, the electric skillet is a remarkable vehicle for getting it on the table fast and oh so tasty.

Poultry's versatility is its strong suit. Whether you're preparing juicy *Roast Chicken with Garden Vegetables*, *Asian Chicken and Vegetable Stir-Fry*, or *Curried Chicken Breasts*, this chapter will provide you with the right dish for whatever your heart desires. If you favor the most delicate of fare, you'll love *Chicken Piccata*, sauced with lemon and sherry or *Chicken and Shrimp Paella*, an elegant dish with rice and wine. For a full-bodied luscious Italian tomato sauce, you'll want second helpings of *Chicken Cacciatore*.

The electric skillet so easily showcases the many facets of chicken. For a casual dinner with friends or family, let *Chicken Tostadas with Chipotle Salsa* or *Best Chicken Tetrazzini* highlight the evening.

The recipes in this chapter turn chicken into something spectacular. *Ham-Stuffed Chicken Breasts* will turn heads, and you don't have to wait for a holiday to feature *Baked Turkey Breast*. Both are festive, delectable, and easy enough for everyday.

Roast Chicken with Garden Vegetables

4	tablespoons vegetable oil, divided		1	clove garlic, minced
4	ounces green beans, ends trimmed		¼	teaspoon dried basil leaves
4	ounces small mushrooms		¼	teaspoon dried marjoram leaves
1	small zucchini, sliced diagonally		¼	teaspoon dried rosemary leaves
	into ½-inch pieces (about 1 cup)		¼	teaspoon dried thyme leaves
1	medium red or green pepper,		½	cup dry white wine
	cut into 1-inch pieces (about 1 cup)	1 to 1½	cups water
3	pound roasting chicken		½	teaspoon chicken flavor instant
	Salt and pepper			bouillon
1	medium onion, sliced			Salt and pepper

Heat skillet at 225°. Add 3 tablespoons oil, beans, mushrooms, zucchini, and pepper; cook 2 to 3 minutes, stirring occasionally. Remove vegetables; reserve.

Sprinkle cavity of chicken lightly with salt and pepper. Add remaining 1 tablespoon oil and chicken; cook at 350° until well browned, turning every 2 to 3 minutes. Remove chicken. Add onion and garlic; cook at 225° for 2 minutes. Stir in basil, marjoram, rosemary, and thyme; cook 2 minutes. Return chicken to skillet. Add wine, 1 cup water, and bouillon; cook at 400° until boiling. Reduce heat to simmer, between Warm and 200°; cook, covered, 40 minutes, adding more water if necessary. Add reserved vegetables to skillet; cook, covered, until vegetables are tender and juices in chicken are clear when inside of thigh is pierced with a fork, about 10 minutes. Season vegetables to taste with salt and pepper.

4 to 6 servings

Mustard Baked Chicken

3	pound roasting chicken		2	teaspoons dried chives
	Salt and pepper		1	teaspoon dried tarragon leaves
2	tablespoons vegetable oil		½	cup dry white wine or chicken broth
½	cup Dijon-style mustard		1	tablespoon flour
1	tablespoon melted butter or		1	cup half-and-half
	margarine			

Sprinkle cavity of chicken lightly with salt and pepper. Heat skillet at 350°. Add oil and chicken; cook until well browned, turning every 2 to 3 minutes. Place chicken on rack in skillet. Mix mustard, butter, chives, and tarragon in small bowl; brush 2 tablespoons of mixture on chicken. Pour wine into skillet; cook, covered, at 225°, until chicken is tender and juices are clear when inside of thigh is pierced with a fork, 45 to 50 minutes. Remove chicken to serving platter; keep warm.

Stir remaining mustard mixture, flour, and half-and-half into pan juices; cook at 250° until sauce is thickened, about 5 minutes, stirring constantly.

4 to 6 servings

Traditional Chicken Salad

2	cups chicken broth or stock	½ to ¾	cup mayonnaise
2	4- to 5-inch sprigs fresh thyme (optional)	2	teaspoons Dijon-style mustard
1	bay leaf	2	teaspoons fresh lemon juice
4	boneless skinless chicken breast halves (about 1¼ pounds)	2 to 3	tablespoons chopped fresh tarragon or flat-leaf parsley
2	ribs celery, finely diced		Salt and pepper

Combine broth, thyme, and bay leaf in skillet; heat at 400° until boiling. Add chicken breasts. Reduce heat to simmer, between Warm and 200°. Simmer, covered, until chicken is cooked through, about 10 to 15 minutes. Remove chicken and cool.

Cut chicken into bite-size pieces. Mix chicken, celery, mayonnaise, mustard, lemon juice, tarragon, salt, and pepper to taste in medium bowl. Chill and serve.

Serving Tip: Chicken Salad can be served on a bed of lettuce or in a sandwich. Add any combination of the following ingredients to enhance your Chicken Salad recipe.

Optional Ingredients:

1	cup red grapes, halved	¾	cup sliced almonds, toasted
1	cup mandarin oranges		Curry powder, to taste
¾	cup chopped pecans, toasted		

5 to 6 cups

Ham-Stuffed Chicken Breasts

4	boneless skinless chicken breast halves, (about 1¼ pounds)	2	ounces thinly sliced baked ham
1	cup dry white wine	½	cup shredded Swiss cheese
	Salt and pepper	1	egg white
		1	teaspoon Dijon-style mustard

Pound chicken breasts lightly until even in thickness; place in shallow glass baking dish and pour wine over. Let stand 30 minutes, turning chicken occasionally.

Remove chicken from wine; reserve wine. Season chicken breasts lightly with salt and pepper. Arrange ham on chicken breasts. Mix cheese, egg white, and mustard in small bowl. Spread equal amounts of cheese mixture on ham. Roll up chicken breasts jelly-roll style; secure with toothpicks.

Heat skillet at 300°. Place chicken breasts in skillet; cook, with cover 1 inch ajar, until chicken is browned and juices are clear when thickest parts are pierced with fork, about 8 to 10 minutes. Add reserved wine; cook until wine is nearly evaporated, 4 to 5 minutes, turning chicken to glaze.

4 servings

Mexican Chicken Torta

6 cups water	½ cup roasted tomato salsa, plus additional for serving
2 cloves garlic, minced	1 tablespoon chopped fresh cilantro, plus additional for garnish
½ cup coarsely chopped onion	
½ teaspoon dried oregano leaves	
¾ teaspoon salt, divided	6 flour tortillas (7-inch diameter)
2 bone-in chicken breast halves	2 cups shredded cheddar jack cheese
½ teaspoon ground cumin	Chopped tomato
½ cup black beans, drained, rinsed	Sour cream

Bring water, garlic, onion, oregano, and ½ teaspoon salt to a boil in skillet at 400°. Add chicken breasts. If necessary add additional cup hot water to cover chicken as much as possible. Return to boil, reduce temperature to 300°; simmer, uncovered, 10 minutes, skimming the surface of foam as necessary. Turn skillet off and cover. Let chicken steep 10 minutes. Remove chicken; set aside until cool enough to handle. Remove and discard skin and bones. Shred meat into small strips. Broth can be strained and reserved for another use, if desired.

Season shredded chicken with remaining ¼ teaspoon salt and cumin. Stir in black beans, salsa, and cilantro.

Spray skillet with nonstick cooking spray. Lay one tortilla on skillet; top with ¼ of the chicken mixture and ½ cup of the cheese. Repeat layering, ending with another tortilla. Heat skillet at 250°, cook, covered, 5 minutes. Uncover, spray top tortilla with nonstick cooking spray and carefully turn over torta. Cook, covered, until cheese is melted and filling is hot, about 5 minutes. Remove and keep warm. Make the second torta following the steps above. **Note:** It is not necessary to turn skillet off, but use caution when building the second torta.

Place tortas on serving platter. Top each with tomatoes and cilantro. Cut into wedges and serve with additional salsa and sour cream, as desired.

4 servings

Chicken Tostadas with Chipotle Salsa

Chipotle Salsa (see recipe below)

4 boneless skinless chicken breast halves, cut into ¾-inch pieces (about 1¼ pounds)

1 tablespoon lime juice

1 tablespoon olive oil

1 teaspoon regular or Mexican chili powder

1 teaspoon minced garlic

½ teaspoon ground cumin

½ teaspoon salt

1 16-ounce can refried black beans

2 tablespoons chopped fresh cilantro

2 cups hot cooked rice

8 flat tostadas (5¼-inch diameter)

Assorted toppings, optional:
Shredded Mexican blend cheese
Shredded lettuce
Diced avocado or guacamole
Sour cream

Make Chipotle Salsa; reserve.

Place chicken in shallow glass baking dish. Mix lime juice, oil, chili powder, garlic, cumin, and salt in small bowl. Pour marinade over chicken. Refrigerate, covered, for 30 minutes.

Heat skillet at 350°. Remove chicken from marinade; discard marinade. Sauté chicken until cooked through, about 5 minutes, stirring often. Remove and keep warm.

Reduce heat to 250°. Add refried beans to skillet, stirring pan juice into beans. Cook, until heated through, about 2 minutes. Remove and reserve.

Stir cilantro into rice; reserve.

Spread each tostada with equal amounts of refried beans, rice, chicken, and about 2 tablespoons Chipotle Salsa. Top each with desired toppings and serve with additional salsa.

Shopping Tip: Tostadas can be found in the ethnic section of the supermarket or in a Hispanic market.

8 servings

Chipotle Salsa

2 cups chopped tomatoes (about 3 medium)

⅓ cup chopped onion

¼ cup chopped fresh cilantro

1 tablespoon lime juice

1 tablespoon minced canned chipotle peppers in adobo sauce or chipotle pepper sauce

1 teaspoon minced garlic

½ teaspoon salt

Mix all ingredients in medium bowl. Cover and refrigerate 30 minutes to 2 hours to blend flavors.

About 2⅓ cups

Chicken Hawaiian

- ½ cup all-purpose flour
- 1 teaspoon salt
- ¼ teaspoon pepper
- 6 chicken legs with thighs attached
- 4 tablespoons vegetable oil, divided
- 1½ cups water, divided
- ½ teaspoon chicken flavor instant bouillon
- 2 cups sliced mushrooms
- ½ cup unsweetened pineapple juice
- 1½ tablespoons soy sauce
- ¼ cup cider vinegar
- ¼ cup sugar
- 1 small clove garlic, minced
- 1 tablespoon cornstarch
- 2 tablespoons cold water
- 1 large tomato, cut into wedges
- Salt and pepper
- Hot cooked rice

Combine flour, salt, and pepper in large plastic bag; add chicken; seal bag and shake to coat chicken. Heat skillet at 350°. Add 3 tablespoons oil and chicken; cook until golden, about 5 minutes on each side. Pour excess drippings from skillet. Add 1 cup water and bouillon; cook at 400° until boiling. Reduce heat to simmer, between Warm and 200°; cook, covered, until chicken is tender and juices are clear when thickest parts are pierced with a fork, about 30 minutes. Remove chicken; keep warm. Clean skillet.

Heat skillet at 225°. Add remaining tablespoon oil and mushrooms; cook 1 minute. Stir in pineapple juice, remaining ½ cup water, soy sauce, vinegar, sugar, and garlic; cook at 400° until boiling. Reduce heat to simmer, between Warm and 200°. Mix cornstarch and cold water. Stir into pineapple juice mixture; cook until thickened, about 1 minute, stirring constantly. Stir in tomato; cook 1 minute. Season to taste with salt and pepper. Serve chicken on rice. Spoon sauce over chicken.

6 servings

Chicken and Shrimp Paella

- 1 tablespoon olive oil
- 4 ounces Italian sausage, cut into ½-inch pieces
- 1 cup chopped red pepper
- ½ cup chopped onion
- 2 cloves garlic, minced
- 4 boneless skinless chicken breast halves (about 1¼ pounds)
- 1 cup medium grain rice
- 2½ cups chicken broth
- ½ cup dry white wine
- ¼ teaspoon crumbled saffron threads
- ¼ teaspoon salt
- 8 ounces shrimp, peeled, deveined
- ½ cup frozen peas

Heat oil in skillet at 300°. Add sausage, pepper, onion, and garlic; sauté until onion is tender, about 2 to 3 minutes. Remove. Add chicken; cook until browned, about 1 minute per side. Add sausage and vegetable mixture, rice, broth, wine, saffron, and salt; cook at 400° until boiling. Reduce heat to simmer, between Warm and 200°; cook, covered, 20 minutes. Stir in shrimp and peas; cook, covered, until shrimp is pink, about 3 to 4 minutes. Turn heat to OFF; let stand 5 minutes before serving.

4 servings

Chicken Creole

2	tablespoons butter	1½	cups water	
⅔	cup chopped green pepper	2	teaspoons chicken flavor instant bouillon	
½	cup chopped onion			
½	cup chopped celery	1	tablespoon minced parsley	
2	cloves garlic, minced	½ to 1	teaspoon crushed red pepper	
½	cup all-purpose flour	½	teaspoon dried basil leaves	
1	teaspoon salt	½	teaspoon dried thyme leaves	
1	teaspoon pepper	4	cups cubed cooked chicken	
2	14½-ounce cans diced tomatoes		Hot cooked rice	

Heat butter in skillet at Warm until melted. Add green pepper, onion, celery, and garlic; cook at 225° until vegetables are tender, about 4 minutes. Stir in flour, salt, and pepper; cook until flour is light brown, about 5 minutes, stirring frequently. Stir in tomatoes, water, bouillon, parsley, red pepper, basil, and thyme; cook at 400° until boiling. Reduce heat to simmer, between Warm and 200°; cook until slightly thickened, 10 to 15 minutes, stirring occasionally. Stir in chicken; cook, covered, 5 minutes. Serve with rice.

6 servings

Chicken Cacciatore

1	14-ounce can chicken broth	3	tablespoons olive oil
1	6-ounce can tomato paste	1	large onion, minced
½	cup dry white wine	1	large green pepper, cut into ½-inch pieces
1	teaspoon dried basil leaves		
1	teaspoon dried oregano leaves	8	ounces sliced mushrooms
1	clove garlic, minced		Hot cooked pasta
3½	pounds skinless chicken pieces		Chopped fresh parsley
	Flour		

Mix chicken broth, tomato paste, wine, basil, oregano, and garlic in small bowl. Reserve.

Coat chicken with flour. Heat oil in skillet at 350°. Add chicken, onion, and pepper; cook until chicken is browned on one side, about 5 minutes. Turn chicken pieces; add mushrooms. Pour tomato paste mixture over chicken pieces; heat until boiling. Reduce heat to simmer, between Warm and 200°. Cook, covered, until chicken is tender and juices are clear when thickest parts are pierced with a fork, about 35 to 40 minutes. Serve chicken and sauce over pasta. Sprinkle with parsley.

4 to 6 servings

Chicken Piccata

4	boneless skinless chicken breast halves (about 1¼ pound) Flour		1	tablespoon vegetable oil Salt and pepper
2	tablespoons butter or margarine		2 to 4	tablespoons dry sherry
			2 to 3	tablespoons lemon juice

Pound chicken breasts lightly to ¼-inch thickness; cut into serving pieces. Coat chicken lightly with flour. Heat butter and oil in skillet at Warm until butter is melted. Add chicken; cook at 350° until browned, 3 to 4 minutes on each side. Remove chicken, sprinkle lightly with salt and pepper.

Add sherry and lemon juice to skillet; cook at 225° until sauce is thickened, scraping drippings from bottom of skillet with plastic or wooden utensil. Return chicken to skillet; cook 2 minutes, turning chicken to coat with sauce. Serve sauce over chicken.

4 servings

Best Chicken Tetrazzini

¼	cup butter or margarine		¼	teaspoon salt
¼	cup all-purpose flour		⅛	teaspoon pepper
2½	cups milk		2	cups cubed cooked chicken (about 1 pound)
1	tablespoon plus 1 teaspoon dry sherry		8	ounces spaghetti, cooked, drained
1	teaspoon chicken flavor instant bouillon		1	4-ounce can sliced mushrooms, drained
1	teaspoon minced parsley		¼	cup grated Parmesan cheese
¼	teaspoon ground nutmeg			

Heat butter in skillet at Warm until melted. Stir in flour; cook at 250° for 3 minutes, stirring constantly. Whisk in milk, cook at 400° until boiling. Reduce heat to 200°; cook until thickened, whisking constantly. Whisk in sherry, bouillon, parsley, nutmeg, salt, and pepper; cook 1 minute. Stir in chicken, spaghetti, mushrooms, and cheese; cook until heated through.

4 servings

Chicken, Asparagus, and Pasta with Sun-Dried Tomato Pesto

Sun-Dried Tomato Pesto
(see recipe below)
4 boneless skinless chicken breast
halves (about 1¼ pounds)
3 tablespoons lemon juice
1 clove garlic, minced

1 tablespoon olive oil, divided
12 ounces asparagus, ends trimmed,
cut into 1½-inch pieces
8 ounces rotini pasta, cooked, drained
Salt and pepper
Parmesan cheese

Make Sun-Dried Tomato Pesto; reserve.

Pound chicken to ½-inch thickness and place in a shallow glass baking dish. Mix lemon juice and garlic in small bowl. Pour lemon mixture over chicken; refrigerate 15 minutes (do not marinate longer).

Heat 1 teaspoon oil in skillet at 275°. Add asparagus; cook until crisp-tender, about 8 to 10 minutes, stirring frequently. Remove and reserve.

Add remaining 2 teaspoons oil to skillet. Remove chicken from marinade; discard marinade. Place chicken in skillet; cook at 300° until it springs back when touched, about 9 to 11 minutes, turning once or twice. Remove and keep warm.

Reduce heat to Warm. Return asparagus to skillet. Add pasta and 2 tablespoons Sun-Dried Tomato Pesto. Toss to coat; season with salt and pepper to taste. Turn heat off. Return chicken to skillet and place on top of pasta, season with salt and pepper and top with remaining pesto. Sprinkle with Parmesan.

4 servings

Sun-Dried Tomato Pesto

2 tablespoons pine nuts
½ cup fresh basil
½ cup chopped sun-dried tomatoes
packed in oil
1 teaspoon minced garlic

½ cup olive oil
1 tablespoon grated Parmesan cheese
½ teaspoon lemon zest
Salt and pepper

Heat skillet at 300°. Add pine nuts; heat until toasted, about 4 minutes, stirring constantly. Remove and cool.

Combine pine nuts, basil, and tomatoes in food processor. Process until chopped. Add garlic; with machine running, gradually add oil; process until smooth. Remove to bowl; stir in Parmesan, lemon zest, salt, and pepper to taste.

About 1⅓ cups

Orange Chicken with Raisins and Almonds

½ cup all-purpose flour	¼ teaspoon ground cinnamon
1 teaspoon salt	⅛ teaspoon ground mace
½ teaspoon ground cinnamon	1 tablespoon almond or orange flavor liqueur (optional)
⅛ teaspoon pepper	
3 tablespoons vegetable oil	2 tablespoons cornstarch
3 to 3½ pounds chicken pieces	¼ cup cold water
3 cups water	Salt and pepper
1½ teaspoons chicken flavor instant bouillon	½ cup golden raisins
Water	¼ cup slivered almonds, toasted
⅔ cup undiluted frozen orange juice concentrate, thawed	**Turmeric Rice** (see recipe below)

Combine flour, salt, cinnamon, and pepper in a large plastic bag; add chicken, seal bag and shake to coat chicken.

Heat skillet at 350°. Add oil and chicken; cook, covered, until browned on all sides, 10 to 15 minutes. Remove chicken; pour excess drippings from skillet. Add water and bouillon; cook at 400° until boiling, scraping drippings from bottom of skillet with plastic or wooden utensil. Return chicken to skillet; reduce heat to simmer, between Warm and 200°; cook, covered, until chicken is tender and juices are clear when thickest parts are pierced with a fork, 30 to 40 minutes. Remove chicken to serving platter; keep warm. Reserve cooking liquid; strain and remove excess fat with baster. Clean skillet.

Add enough water to cooking liquid to make 2½ cups; pour into skillet. Stir in orange juice concentrate, ¼ teaspoon cinnamon, and mace; heat at 400° until boiling. Reduce heat to simmer, between Warm and 200°. Stir in liqueur. Mix cornstarch and cold water; whisk into skillet, whisking constantly until thickened. Season sauce to taste with salt and pepper. Stir in raisins and almonds; cook until heated, about 1 minute. Spoon sauce over chicken; keep warm.

Make Turmeric Rice. Serve with chicken.

4 to 6 servings

Turmeric Rice

2¼ cups enriched precooked rice	1 teaspoon grated orange peel
2¼ cups water	¼ teaspoon ground turmeric
¾ teaspoon salt	Minced parsley
1 tablespoon butter	

Cook rice in skillet according to package directions, using water, salt, and butter. Stir orange peel and turmeric into rice. Remove to bowl; sprinkle with parsley.

4 to 6 servings

Curried Chicken Breasts

2	tablespoons vegetable oil		3	tablespoons flour
6	boneless skinless chicken breast halves (about 2 pounds)		1	14½-ounce can diced tomatoes
1	cup chopped onion		1½	cups water
1	clove garlic, minced		¾	teaspoon chicken flavor instant bouillon
1	teaspoon minced fresh gingerroot		1	medium apple, peeled, cored, cut into 16 slices
1	tablespoon curry powder		¼	cup golden raisins
¼	teaspoon ground cinnamon			Salt
¼	teaspoon dried coriander			Hot cooked rice
⅛	teaspoon ground cumin			Plain yogurt
⅛	teaspoon crushed red pepper			

Heat skillet at 350°. Add oil and chicken; cook until browned, about 2 minutes on each side. Remove chicken. Add onion, garlic, and gingerroot; cook at 225° until onion is tender, about 2 minutes. Stir in curry powder, cinnamon, coriander, cumin, and red pepper; cook 1 minute. Stir in flour; cook 1 minute. Stir in tomatoes, water, and bouillon. Return chicken to skillet; cook at 400° until boiling. Reduce heat to simmer, between Warm and 200°; cook, covered, until chicken springs back when touched, about 15 minutes. Stir in apple and raisins during last 10 minutes of cooking time. Season to taste with salt. Serve chicken with rice. Top with yogurt as desired.

6 servings

Teriyaki Chicken

⅓	cup teriyaki sauce		2	tablespoons peanut oil
⅓	cup sake or dry sherry		1	green onion, sliced diagonally into ¼-inch slices
1	tablespoon cornstarch			Hot cooked rice
2	teaspoons grated grapefruit peel			
1	clove garlic, minced			
4	boneless skinless chicken breast halves, cut into ½-inch pieces (about 1¼ pounds)			

Mix teriyaki sauce, sake, cornstarch, grapefruit peel, and garlic in small bowl; pour over chicken in shallow glass baking dish. Let stand 30 minutes.

Remove chicken from marinade; reserve marinade. Heat oil in skillet at 325°. Add chicken; cook until chicken is tender, about 4 minutes. Stir in reserved marinade; cook until thickened, stirring constantly. Sprinkle with onion. Serve with rice.

4 servings

Asian Chicken and Vegetable Stir-Fry

½	cup peanuts or cashews	1	8-ounce can sliced water chestnuts, drained
1	tablespoon sesame seeds		
3	tablespoons peanut oil	2	green onions, thinly sliced
1	teaspoon sesame oil	2	tablespoons soy sauce
4	boneless skinless chicken breast halves, cut into 1-inch pieces (about 1¼ pounds)	1	teaspoon sugar
		¼	teaspoon pepper
		⅛	teaspoon Chinese 5-spice powder, optional
2½	cups diagonally sliced broccoli		
1	cup sliced red pepper	1	7-ounce jar baby corn, drained
¾	cup diagonally sliced carrots		Hot cooked rice

Heat skillet at 300°. Add peanuts; heat until toasted. Remove and reserve. Add sesame seeds; heat until toasted. Remove and reserve.

Increase heat to 400°. Add oils and chicken; cook until brown. Remove chicken and reserve.

Add broccoli, red pepper, and carrots to skillet; stir-fry 2 minutes. Add water chestnuts and onions; stir-fry 2 minutes. Mix soy sauce, sugar, pepper, and 5-spice powder in small bowl; stir into vegetable mixture in skillet. Add baby corn and reserved chicken; cook, covered, until vegetables are crisp-tender, 2 to 4 minutes. Sprinkle with reserved peanuts and sesame seeds. Serve with rice.

Shopping Tip: Chinese 5-spice powder can be found at Asian markets or most supermarkets.

6 servings

Sesame Ginger Chicken

1	cup fresh breadcrumbs	2	tablespoons minced fresh gingerroot
2	tablespoons sesame seeds	2	tablespoons honey
1	egg white	3	cloves garlic, minced
¼	cup plus 1 tablespoon soy sauce, divided	1	tablespoon seasoned rice wine vinegar
4	boneless skinless chicken breast halves (about 1¼ pounds)	1	teaspoon sesame oil
½	cup orange juice	1 to 1½	tablespoons vegetable oil, divided
¼	cup thinly sliced green onions	1	teaspoon cornstarch
		1	tablespoon water

Heat skillet at 250°. Add breadcrumbs and sesame seeds; cook until breadcrumbs and some sesame seeds begin to brown, about 5 to 6 minutes, stirring constantly. Remove to shallow bowl; reserve.

Combine egg white and 1 tablespoon soy sauce in another shallow bowl; beat lightly. Reserve.

Pound chicken breasts lightly to ½-inch thickness. Dip chicken in egg white mixture, then roll in breadcrumb mixture to coat evenly. Set each on a baking sheet as they are coated.

Mix orange juice, onions, remaining ¼ cup soy sauce, ginger, honey, garlic, vinegar, and sesame oil in small bowl. Reserve.

Heat 1 tablespoon oil in skillet at 350°. Add chicken; cook until chicken springs back when touched, about 9 to 11 minutes, turning every 3 minutes. Add remaining ½ tablespoon oil as necessary. Remove chicken to serving plate; keep warm.

Pour orange juice mixture into skillet. Mix cornstarch and water in small bowl. Stir into orange juice mixture; bring to a boil. Cook until sauce is thickened, about 30 to 60 seconds, stirring constantly.

Serve sauce with chicken.

4 servings

Preparation Tip: *If chicken breasts are large after pounding, cut in half lengthwise to facilitate coating.*

Lemon Chicken

⅓	cup sugar		2	tablespoons peanut or vegetable oil
1	tablespoon cornstarch		2	cups snow peas
¼	cup lemon juice		1	cup thinly sliced carrots
¼	cup rice wine vinegar or distilled white vinegar		½	cup water
1	teaspoon soy sauce		¼	teaspoon chicken flavor instant bouillon
1	teaspoon grated lemon peel		½	cup blanched whole almonds
4	boneless skinless chicken breast halves, cut into 1-inch pieces (about 1¼ pounds)		¼	cup thinly sliced green onions
				Salt and pepper
				Hot cooked rice

Mix sugar, cornstarch, lemon juice, vinegar, soy sauce, and lemon peel in small bowl; pour over chicken in shallow glass baking dish. Let stand 15 minutes.

Remove chicken from marinade, reserve marinade. Heat oil in skillet at 350°. Add chicken; stir-fry until brown, about 4 minutes. Remove chicken from skillet; reserve. Add snow peas and carrots; stir-fry 2 minutes. Stir in reserved marinade, water, and bouillon; heat at 400° until boiling. Reduce heat to simmer, between Warm and 200°; cook until sauce is thickened, about 2 minutes, stirring constantly.

Stir in reserved chicken, almonds, and onions; cook until heated, about 2 minutes. Season to taste with salt and pepper. Serve with rice.

4 servings

Braised Turkey Legs

3	tablespoons vegetable oil		1½	teaspoons chicken flavor instant bouillon
2	turkey legs			
	Salt and pepper		½	teaspoon dried sage leaves
2	cups water		½	teaspoon dried rosemary leaves

Heat skillet at 350°. Add oil and turkey legs; cook, covered, until well browned, 10 to 12 minutes. Remove turkey legs; sprinkle lightly with salt and pepper. Add water, bouillon, sage, and rosemary to skillet; heat at 400° until boiling. Reduce heat to simmer, between Warm and 200°. Place turkey legs on rack in skillet; cook, covered, until turkey legs are tender and juices are clear when thickest parts are pierced with a fork, 1¼ to 1½ hours.

2 servings

Chinese Chicken Salad

2	cups water		3	tablespoons honey
¼	cup dry sherry		¾	cup diagonally sliced green onions
2	teaspoons chicken flavor instant bouillon		3	cloves garlic, minced
6	chicken breast halves (about ½ pound each)		½	teaspoon ground ginger
			3	cups finely sliced Chinese or green cabbage
1	tablespoon Szechwan peppercorns, lightly crushed		1	8-ounce can sliced water chestnuts, drained
3	tablespoons vegetable oil		1	red or green pepper, cut into thin strips
3	tablespoons rice wine vinegar			
3	tablespoons soy sauce			

Heat water, sherry, and bouillon in skillet at 400° until boiling. Add chicken; reduce heat to simmer, between Warm and 200°. Cook, covered, until chicken is tender and juices are clear when thickest parts are pierced with a fork, about 20 minutes. Remove chicken; set aside until cool enough to handle. Discard cooking liquid. Remove and discard skin and bones from chicken. Shred chicken coarsely; keep warm.

Heat skillet at 225°. Add peppercorns; cook until toasted, about 2 minutes, stirring frequently. Add oil, vinegar, soy sauce, honey, onions, garlic, and ginger; cook at Warm, 2 minutes. Stir in chicken, cabbage, water chestnuts, and pepper; toss. Serve immediately.

4 servings

Baked Turkey Breast

4½ to 5	pound turkey breast		2	cups water
	Vegetable oil		1	teaspoon chicken flavor instant bouillon
	Salt and pepper			

Lightly brush turkey breast with oil; sprinkle cavity of turkey lightly with salt and pepper. Insert meat thermometer so that tip is centered in thickest part of breast, away from bone. Place turkey breast on rack in skillet. Add water and bouillon; heat at 400° until boiling. Reduce heat to 325°; cook, covered, 30 minutes. Reduce heat to 275°; cook, covered, until thermometer in turkey breast registers 170°, about 1¼ to 1½ hours. Remove turkey breast to serving platter. Let stand for 15 minutes before slicing, loosely covered with aluminum foil.

8 to 10 servings

Apricot-Honey Glazed Duckling

4	pound frozen duckling, thawed, cut into fourths	½	cup apricot preserves
	Salt and pepper	2	tablespoons honey
1	cup water	2	tablespoons lemon juice
½	teaspoon chicken flavor instant bouillon	½	teaspoon grated lemon peel

Generously pierce skin of duckling pieces with fork. Heat skillet at 350°. Add duckling; cook, covered, until well browned, about 8 minutes on each side. Remove duckling from skillet; sprinkle lightly with salt and pepper. Pour excess drippings from skillet.

Place duckling pieces, skin sides up, on rack in skillet. Add water and bouillon; heat at 400° until water is boiling. Reduce heat to simmer, between Warm and 200°; cook, covered, until duckling is tender and juices are clear when thickest parts are pierced with a fork, about 1¼ to 1¾ hours. Remove duckling from skillet. Clean skillet.

Mix preserves, honey, lemon juice, and lemon peel in skillet; cook at 225° until bubbly. Add duckling with skin-side down, coating pieces evenly with glaze; cook, covered, until glaze is thickened and duckling is golden, about 5 minutes.

4 servings

Cornish Hens with Orange-Curry Sauce

2	1-pound Cornish hens	¼	teaspoon ground cinnamon
	Garlic powder	1	cup orange juice
	Salt and pepper	1	tablespoon light rum (optional)
2	tablespoons vegetable oil	1	tablespoon butter
½	cup finely chopped onion	1	teaspoon light brown sugar
1	clove garlic, minced		Salt and pepper
1	teaspoon curry powder		

Sprinkle cavities of hens lightly with garlic powder, salt, and pepper. Heat skillet at 350°. Add oil and hens; cook, covered, until golden, about 4 minutes on each side. Remove hens from skillet; pour off excess drippings, reserving 1 tablespoon in skillet.

Add onion, garlic, curry powder, and cinnamon; cook at 225° for 2 minutes. Stir in orange juice and rum; cook at 400° until boiling. Add hens to skillet. Reduce heat to simmer, between Warm and 200°; cook, covered, until hens are tender and juices are clear when thickest parts are pierced with a fork, about 45 minutes. Remove hens to serving platter; keep warm.

Stir butter and sugar into skillet. Season sauce to taste with salt and pepper. Serve sauce with hens.

2 servings

CHAPTER EIGHT
Fish & Seafood

The need for fast meals that are healthy, nutritious, and light has made fish and seafood an increasingly popular choice. Almost all types of fish provide fewer calories and less cholesterol than equivalent portions of meat. Most fish and seafood take only minutes to cook, making them the hero for frenzied mealtimes.

All fishermen know the joy of pan-fried fresh fish. Whether your "catch" is fresh or from the market, you'll find many great recipes in this chapter. The classic preparation applied to *Southern-Style Fried Catfish* can be used on any small freshwater fish. The mild and flaky *Tilapia with Olive-Orange Butter* will surprise you with its speed of preparation and its most delightful flavor. *Pepper-Seared Salmon Fillets* is a tantalizing treat for the palate. And, for those times when a little indulgence is in order, the *Spice-Rubbed Tuna with Fruit Salsa* will oblige nicely.

Steaming and poaching are excellent ways to highlight the delicacy of fish and seafood. The electric skillet not only takes the guesswork out of these techniques but also makes fast work of the light sauces that go so well with them. You'll find *Steamed Trout with Red Pepper Sauce* and *Tilapia Fillets with Shrimp Mousse*, both show-stoppers when company's coming. *Cioppino* is a wonderful Italian fish stew to savor while cozying up to a fire on a chilly night.

You'll discover many techniques for preparing wonderful meals with fish and seafood. Keep in mind that you can substitute frozen fish for fresh in the recipes. Simply thaw the fish in the refrigerator or in a bowl of cold water until it's not quite completely defrosted—it should still be cold and firm. Then rinse off any remaining ice crystals and pat dry with paper toweling.

Asian Steamed Fish

1	dressed whole whitefish or other freshwater fish (about 2 pounds)		1	teaspoon slivered fresh gingerroot
1	teaspoon salt		1	clove garlic, thinly sliced
2	slices fresh gingerroot (about size of dime)		3	tablespoons teriyaki sauce
	Water		3	tablespoons sake or dry white wine
3	tablespoons peanut oil		1	teaspoon sesame oil
			1	teaspoon light brown sugar
			2	green onions, sliced

Rub fish, inside and out, with salt and 2 slices gingerroot; discard gingerroot. Place fish on rack in skillet. Add 1½ inches water to skillet; heat at 400° until boiling. Reduce heat to simmer, between Warm and 200°; cook, covered until fish is tender and flakes with a fork, about 12 minutes. Remove fish to serving platter; keep warm. Discard water; clean skillet.

Heat skillet at 225°. Add oil, slivered gingerroot, and garlic; stir-fry 2 minutes. Spoon mixture over fish. Combine teriyaki sauce, sake, sesame oil, and sugar in skillet; cook 1 minute. Pour over fish; sprinkle with green onions.

4 servings

Southern-Style Fried Catfish

¼	cup white self-rising cornmeal		4	4- to 6-ounce catfish fillets
¼	cup all-purpose flour		1	egg, beaten
½	teaspoon salt		2	tablespoons milk
¼	teaspoon white pepper		3	tablespoons vegetable oil
⅛	teaspoon cayenne pepper			

Combine cornmeal, flour, salt, pepper, and cayenne pepper in small shallow bowl. Coat catfish with seasoned cornmeal mixture. Combine egg and milk in another small shallow bowl. Dip fish in egg mixture; coat fish again with cornmeal mixture. Heat oil in skillet at 300°. Add fish; cook until golden and crisp, about 3 minutes on each side.

4 servings

Trout with Roasted Garlic Sauce

1 medium garlic bulb (about 20 cloves)	¼ cup all-purpose flour
1 tablespoons olive oil	¼ teaspoon salt
¼ cup butter or margarine, divided	⅛ teaspoon white pepper
2 tablespoons finely chopped onion	4 5-ounce whole dressed Rocky Mountain or other fresh water trout
2 tablespoons finely chopped green onions	2 tablespoons vegetable oil

Break cloves apart from garlic bulb, leaving a layer of papery skin surrounding each clove. Heat skillet at 250°. Toss garlic and oil together in skillet until garlic is coated with oil. Cook until garlic is soft, about 20 minutes for small cloves and 30 minutes for large, stirring frequently. Remove cloves; let stand until cool enough to handle. Remove papery skin from roasted cloves. Chop cloves into a paste; reserve. Wipe skillet clean with paper towel.

Heat 2 tablespoons butter in skillet at Warm until melted. Add onions; cook at 225° until onions are soft, about 6 minutes, stirring frequently. Add remaining 2 tablespoons butter and garlic paste, cook 4 minutes. Remove garlic mixture; reserve. Clean skillet.

Combine flour, salt, and pepper in shallow bowl. Coat fish lightly with seasoned flour. Heat oil in skillet at 350°. Add fish; cook, covered, until fish is tender and flakes with a fork, about 3 minutes on each side. Spoon garlic mixture over fish; cook, covered, until heated through, about 1 minute.

4 servings

Steamed Trout with Red Pepper Sauce

2 tablespoons butter, divided	¼ teaspoon anise seed, crushed
½ cup finely chopped red pepper	2 dressed whole rainbow trout or other freshwater trout (about 12 ounces each)
¼ cup thinly sliced green onions	Salt and pepper
1½ cups dry white wine	1 tablespoon sour cream
1 teaspoon lemon juice	

Heat 1 tablespoon butter in skillet at Warm until melted. Add red pepper and onions; cook at 225° for 2 minutes. Stir in wine, lemon juice, and anise; heat at 400° until boiling. Reduce heat to simmer, between Warm and 200°. Sprinkle cavities of fish lightly with salt and pepper. Place on rack in skillet; cook, covered, until fish is tender and flakes with a fork, about 10 minutes. Remove fish to serving platter; keep warm.

Whisk remaining 1 tablespoon butter vigorously into cooking liquid. Turn heat to Off; whisk in sour cream. Serve sauce over fish.

4 servings

Sole Florentine with Mornay Sauce

5	tablespoons butter or margarine, divided			Salt and pepper
2	10-ounce packages frozen chopped spinach, thawed and squeezed dry		½	cup dry sherry
			3	tablespoons lemon juice
2	tablespoons minced onion		2	tablespoons flour
¼	teaspoon ground nutmeg, divided		⅔	cup water
			¼	cup half-and-half
¼	teaspoon salt		1	teaspoon Dijon-style mustard
⅛	teaspoon pepper		½	cup shredded Swiss cheese
1	pound sole fillets			Paprika
				Lemon slices

Heat 2 tablespoons butter in skillet at Warm until melted. Stir in spinach and onion; cook at 225° for 2 minutes. Stir in ⅛ teaspoon nutmeg, salt, and pepper. Spoon spinach mixture on serving platter; keep warm. Clean skillet.

Fold fish fillets lengthwise in half; sprinkle with salt and pepper. Heat sherry, lemon juice, and 1 tablespoon butter in skillet at 400° until boiling. Reduce heat to simmer, between Warm and 200°. Add fish; cook, covered, until fish is tender and flakes with a fork, about 5 minutes. Remove fish and arrange on spinach mixture; keep warm. Pour cooking liquid from skillet into small bowl; reserve.

Heat remaining 2 tablespoons butter in skillet at Warm until melted. Stir in flour; cook 1 minute. Stir in water and reserved cooking liquid; cook at 400° until boiling, stirring constantly. Reduce heat to 200°; stir in half-and-half, mustard, and remaining ⅛ teaspoon nutmeg. Add cheese, stirring until melted. Serve sauce over fish. Sprinkle with paprika; garnish with lemon slices.

4 servings

Tilapia Fillets with Shrimp Mousse

8	ounces uncooked shrimp, peeled, deveined	1	teaspoon salt	
1	tablespoon minced parsley	¼	teaspoon anise seed	
¼	teaspoon paprika	3	whole black peppercorns	
⅛	teaspoon white pepper	1	whole clove	
1	egg white	⅓	cup butter	
¼	cup half-and-half	2	tablespoons all-purpose flour	
4	6- to 8-ounce tilapia fillets	1	cup boiling water	
2	cups water	1 to 2	tablespoons lemon juice	
2	cups dry white wine	½	teaspoon salt	
1	cup sliced onion	¼	teaspoon Dijon-style mustard	
4	lemon slices	⅛	teaspoon white pepper	

Place shrimp, parsley, paprika, and pepper in food processor or blender; process until shrimp is finely ground. Add egg; process 1 minute. With machine running, slowly add half-and-half, process until thoroughly incorporated.

Spread shrimp mixture on fillets, leaving ½ inch margin along sides of fish. Roll up fillets jelly-roll style; secure ends with toothpicks.

Add water, wine, onion, lemon, salt, anise, peppercorns, and clove to skillet. Cook at 400° until boiling. Reduce heat to simmer, between Warm and 200°. Add fish rolls; cook until fish is tender and flakes with a fork, about 8 minutes. Remove fish and keep warm. Discard cooking liquid. Clean skillet.

Heat butter in skillet at Warm until melted. Stir in flour; cook 1 minute. Whisk in boiling water; cook at 200° until slightly thickened, about 5 minutes, whisking constantly. Whisk in lemon juice, salt, mustard, and pepper. Serve over fish.

4 servings

Tilapia with Olive-Orange Butter

¼ cup unsalted butter, softened	1 teaspoon fresh orange juice
2 sun-dried tomatoes, finely chopped	½ teaspoon finely chopped fresh rosemary
2 teaspoons minced pitted kalamata olives	4 6- to 8-ounce tilapia fillets
2 teaspoons minced dried capers	Salt and pepper
1 teaspoon grated orange peel	Flour
	1 tablespoon canola or vegetable oil

Mix butter, tomatoes, olives, capers, orange peel, orange juice, and rosemary in small bowl. Reserve.

Pat fish dry. Season with salt and pepper. Coat lightly with flour, shaking off excess. Heat oil in skillet at 350°. Add fish; cook until golden, about 4 to 5 minutes, turning once halfway through cooking.

Serve flavored butter over fish.

Preparation Tip: Flavored butter may be shaped into a log and frozen for up to 3 months.

4 servings

Red Snapper with Tomato-Jalapeño Sauce

2 pound whole dressed red snapper	½ cup sliced black olives
Salt and pepper	1 tablespoon seeded chopped jalapeño pepper
¼ cup lime juice	2 teaspoons drained capers
2 tablespoons vegetable oil	1 tablespoon chopped fresh cilantro
2 cups sliced onions	½ teaspoon salt
2 cloves garlic, minced	
2 14½-ounce cans diced tomatoes	

Score skin on both sides of fish diagonally, using sharp knife. Season fish lightly with salt and pepper; place in shallow glass baking dish. Pour lime juice over fish; let stand 30 minutes, turning fish occasionally.

Heat skillet at 225°. Add oil, onions, and garlic; cook until tender, about 3 minutes. Stir in remaining ingredients; cook at 400° until boiling. Reduce heat to simmer, between Warm and 200°; cook 3 minutes, stirring frequently. Add fish to skillet; spoon sauce over. Cook with cover ½ inch ajar, basting with sauce occasionally. Turn fish over; continue cooking with cover ½ inch ajar, until fish is tender and flakes with a fork, 20 to 30 minutes.

4 to 6 servings

Spice-Rubbed Tuna with Fruit Salsa

Fruit Salsa (see recipe below)

1½ teaspoons coriander seeds

1 tablespoon paprika

2 teaspoons ground cumin

2 teaspoons sugar

1½ teaspoons ground cayenne pepper

1½ teaspoons ground turmeric

1½ teaspoons freshly ground black pepper

1 teaspoon kosher salt

1 teaspoon ground ginger

4 5- to 6-ounce tuna steaks

2 tablespoons plus 2 teaspoons olive oil, divided

Make Fruit Salsa; reserve.

Heat skillet at 350°. Add coriander; heat until toasted, about 5 minutes. Remove and cool. Grind in spice mill or coffee grinder. Transfer to small bowl; add paprika, cumin, sugar, cayenne pepper, turmeric, pepper, salt, and ginger.

Rub tuna steaks lightly with 2 teaspoons oil. Coat generously with spice rub on both sides. Heat remaining 2 tablespoons oil in skillet at 400°. Sear tuna for 1 to 4 minutes on each side for rare to medium. Serve tuna topped with Fruit Salsa.

4 servings

Fruit Salsa

½ pineapple, peeled, cored, cut into small dice (about 2 cups)

1 nectarine, halved, pitted, cut into small dice

1 kiwi, peeled, cut into small dice

1 plum, halved, pitted, cut into small dice

¼ cup finely chopped red onion

1 jalapeño pepper, seeds and membrane removed, minced

2 tablespoons coarsely chopped fresh mint

1 tablespoon olive oil

1 to 2 tablespoons fresh lime juice, to taste

1 teaspoon honey

Combine all ingredients in medium bowl. Cover; let stand to allow flavors to blend.

Preparation Tip: *Salsa can be made several hours in advance and refrigerated.*

About 3½ cups

Poached Salmon with Yogurt-Dill Sauce

1 6-ounce container plain nonfat or lowfat yogurt, drained of liquid
1 teaspoon lemon juice
1 teaspoon minced garlic
¼ teaspoon dried dill weed
¼ teaspoon salt
⅛ teaspoon pepper

2 cups white wine
2 cups water
2 teaspoons chicken flavor instant bouillon
¼ cup chopped onion
8 whole black peppercorns
4 6-ounce salmon fillets, 1 inch thick

Combine yogurt, lemon juice, garlic, dill weed, salt, and pepper in small bowl. Reserve.

Combine wine, water, bouillon, onion, and peppercorns in skillet; heat at 400° until boiling. Reduce heat to simmer; between Warm and 200°; cook, covered, 5 minutes. Add salmon; cook, covered, until it just flakes, about 4 to 5 minutes. Serve reserved sauce over salmon.

4 servings

Pepper-Seared Salmon Fillets

¼ cup tamari or soy sauce
½ tablespoon fresh orange juice
2 garlic cloves, minced
2 teaspoons honey

2 8-ounce salmon fillets
½ to 1½ tablespoons coarsely ground mixed peppercorns (black, white, pink)
1½ tablespoons olive oil

Combine tamari, orange juice, garlic, and honey in shallow glass baking dish. Add salmon, turning to coat. Refrigerate, covered, 30 minutes, turning occasionally.

Remove salmon from marinade; discard marinade. Pat salmon dry. Coat the flesh-side of fillets with pepper mixture. Use less, if a more subtle heat is desired. Heat oil in skillet at 350° until hot, but not smoking. Cook salmon, pepper-side first, until it just flakes, 3 to 5 minutes on each side.

4 servings

Sweet and Sour Shrimp

3   tablespoons vegetable oil, divided
1   pound uncooked shrimp,
      peeled, deveined
      Cornstarch
1   large green pepper, cut into
      1-inch pieces
¼   cup finely chopped onion
¼   cup drained canned bamboo
      shoots
1   clove garlic, minced
1   teaspoon minced fresh
      gingerroot

1   15¼-ounce can pineapple tidbits,
      drained, juice reserved
¼   cup rice wine vinegar or distilled
      white vinegar
2   teaspoons soy sauce
½   teaspoon sesame oil (optional)
3   tablespoons sugar
1   tablespoon cornstarch
2   tablespoons cold water
1   large tomato, cut into wedges
      Salt
      Hot cooked rice

Heat 2 tablespoons vegetable oil in skillet at 350°. Coat shrimp lightly with cornstarch; cook in skillet until browned, about 2 minutes on each side. Remove shrimp; reserve. Clean skillet.

Heat skillet at 225°. Add remaining 1 tablespoon oil, green pepper, onion, bamboo shoots, garlic, and gingerroot; stir-fry 2 minutes. Stir in reserved pineapple juice, vinegar, soy sauce, sesame oil, and sugar; heat at 400° until boiling. Reduce heat to simmer, between Warm and 200°. Mix cornstarch and water in small bowl; stir into skillet. Cook until thickened, stirring constantly. Stir in reserved shrimp, pineapple, and tomato; cook until heated, about 2 minutes. Season to taste with salt. Serve with rice.

Substitution Tip: 1 pound cod fillets can be substituted for the shrimp. Cut cod into 1-inch pieces; press lightly with paper toweling to remove excess moisture. Coat lightly with cornstarch; cook as above.

4 to 6 servings

Shrimp with Spinach Pesto

Spinach Pesto (see recipe below)
1 tablespoon olive oil
1 pound uncooked shrimp, peeled, deveined
½ cup dry white wine
2 tablespoons lemon juice
¼ teaspoon salt
¼ teaspoon pepper
3 cups hot cooked rice or spaghetti
2 tablespoons grated Parmesan cheese

Make Spinach Pesto; reserve.

Heat oil in skillet at 325°. Add shrimp; cook until shrimp are pink and done, 2 to 3 minutes. Stir in wine and lemon juice; cook at 400° until liquid is nearly evaporated, about 2 minutes. Reduce heat to 200°. Stir in salt, pepper, and Spinach Pesto; cook, covered, until heated, about 2 minutes. Serve over rice or spaghetti; sprinkle with Parmesan cheese.

4 servings

Spinach Pesto

¼ 10-ounce package frozen chopped spinach, thawed and squeezed dry
½ cup olive oil
¼ cup walnuts
2 tablespoons fresh basil leaves
1 clove garlic, minced
⅛ teaspoon salt
⅛ teaspoon pepper

Add spinach, oil, walnuts, basil, garlic, salt, and pepper in food processor or blender. Process until smooth.

About ¾ cup

Seafood and Shrimp Newburg

½	cup butter or margarine		¼	teaspoon white pepper
½	cup sliced mushrooms		⅛	teaspoon ground nutmeg
¼	cup chopped onion		2	pounds skinless cod or other white
½	cup all-purpose flour			fish fillets, cut into ¾-inch pieces
4	cups milk		4	ounces cooked shrimp, peeled,
1	tablespoon dry sherry			deveined, cut in half lengthwise
1	teaspoon salt			Hot cooked rice

Heat butter in skillet at Warm until melted. Add mushrooms and onion; cook at 225° until tender, about 4 minutes. Stir in flour; cook 1 minute, stirring frequently. Gradually stir in milk; cook at 400° until boiling and thickened, stirring constantly. Stir in sherry, salt, pepper, and nutmeg; reduce heat to 250°. Stir in fish and shrimp; cook, covered, until fish is tender and flakes with a fork, 3 to 5 minutes. Serve with rice.

6 servings

Crab Cakes

6	ounces fresh, frozen, or		¼	teaspoon salt
	canned snow crab meat		¼	teaspoon pepper
1	egg, beaten		⅛ to ¼	teaspoon cayenne pepper
2	tablespoons minced celery		⅓	cup crushed saltines
1	tablespoon minced onion			Vegetable oil
1	tablespoon mayonnaise			Tartar sauce
3	drops hot pepper sauce			

Mix crab, egg, celery, onion, mayonnaise, pepper sauce, salt, pepper, and cayenne pepper in medium bowl. Mix in half the saltines. Form crab mixture into 4 patties; coat with remaining saltines. Refrigerate crab cakes 1 hour.

Heat ¼-inch oil in skillet at 325°. Add crab cakes; cook until golden, 2 to 3 minutes on each side. Serve hot with tartar sauce.

2 servings

Seared Scallops with Asian Vegetables

2	tablespoons fresh orange or tangerine juice		2	tablespoons sesame seeds
2	tablespoons tamari or soy sauce		1 to 1½	tablespoons peanut oil, divided
1	tablespoon rice wine or dry sherry		½	medium head bok choy, sliced crosswise in ½-inch pieces
1	teaspoon honey		1	cup sliced shiitake mushrooms
1	teaspoon sesame oil		1	tablespoon minced fresh gingerroot
2	teaspoons grated orange peel		2	garlic cloves, minced
10	large sea scallops, tough muscle removed from side, if necessary		1	green onion, cut into ¼-inch slices Hot cooked rice

Combine orange juice, tamari, wine, honey, oil, and orange peel in shallow glass baking dish. Add scallops; refrigerate for 30 minutes. Remove scallops from marinade; reserve marinade.

Pat scallops dry. Dip one side of each scallop in sesame seeds to coat. Heat 1 tablespoon peanut oil in skillet at 300° until hot, but not smoking. Place scallops sesame-side down in oil. Cook until just opaque in center, about 2 to 4 minutes, turning once. (Use caution, loose sesame seeds tend to jump around in heat of skillet). Remove scallops and keep warm.

Add remaining ½ tablespoon peanut oil to skillet if needed. Add bok choy stalks, mushrooms, gingerroot, garlic, and onion; stir-fry about 3 minutes. Add bok choy greens and reserved marinade; stir-fry 1 minute. Cover; heat for 1 minute. Add scallops, sesame side up, until warmed. Serve immediately with rice.

2 servings

Steamed Shore Dinner

2	tablespoons olive oil			Salt and pepper
1	large onion, coarsely chopped		3	small red potatoes, quartered
2	garlic cloves, minced		2	ears corn, cut into 2-inch pieces
1	bay leaf		¾ to 1	pound red snapper, cod, or halibut
1	teaspoon dried oregano leaves, crumbled			fillets, cut into 2-inch pieces
½	cup white wine		12	tail-on medium shrimp, peeled, deveined
2	14½-ounce cans fire-roasted or regular diced tomatoes		12	mussels, scrubbed, de-bearded
1	cup reduced-sodium chicken broth		2	tablespoons chopped fresh flat-leaf parsley
1	teaspoon grated orange peel		2	tablespoons sliced fresh basil

Heat olive oil in skillet at 225°. Sauté onion, garlic, bay leaf, and oregano until onions are tender, about 3 to 5 minutes. Add wine; boil until reduced by half, about 1 to 2 minutes. Add tomatoes, broth, orange peel, and salt and pepper to taste; heat until boiling. Reduce heat to simmer, between Warm and 200°; cook, stirring occasionally, until liquid becomes saucelike, about 10 minutes. Add potatoes; cook, covered, about 8 minutes. Add corn and fish; cook, covered, about 3 minutes. Add shrimp and mussels; cook, covered until tender, about 5 minutes. Discard bay leaf and any mussels that have not opened. Sprinkle on parsley and basil. Serve immediately in large soup bowls.

4 servings

Cioppino *(Fish Stew)*

3 tablespoons olive or vegetable oil	1 8-ounce can tomato sauce
1 cup chopped onion	1 cup dry white wine
2 cloves garlic, minced	3 tablespoons minced fresh parsley
1½ cups chopped green pepper	1 teaspoon sugar
1 teaspoon dried basil leaves	¼ teaspoon salt
¼ teaspoon dried oregano leaves	¼ teaspoon pepper
⅛ teaspoon cayenne pepper	6 cherrystone clams (optional)
1 star anise (optional)	8 ounces shrimp, peeled, deveined
1 small bay leaf	1 pound cod or other white fish
2 14½-ounce cans diced tomatoes	fillets, cut into 2-inch pieces

Heat skillet at 225°. Add oil, onion, and garlic; cook 2 minutes. Add green pepper; cook 2 minutes. Stir in basil, oregano, cayenne pepper, anise, and bay leaf; cook 1 minute. Add tomatoes, tomato sauce, wine, parsley, sugar, salt, and pepper; cook at 400° until boiling. Reduce heat to simmer, between Warm and 200°; cook, covered, 30 minutes. Stir in clams; cook, covered, 5 minutes. Add shrimp and cod; cook, covered, until cod is tender and flakes with a fork, about 5 minutes. Serve in bowls.

6 servings

Main Dishes

A hearty casserole, a steaming jambalaya, an irresistible stew, and a cheesy deep-pan pizza never fail to kindle mealtime comfort. With their fused flavors and rich aromas, one-pan main dishes can be the most satisfying of cuisine. On busy days, these culinary opportunities are also a cook's best ally. They need minimal accompaniment, there's only one pan to clean, and almost every dish can be reheated a day or two later with excellent results.

The mellow and comforting taste of *Beef Vegetable Stew with Dill Dumplings* will satisfy the soul on a cold and blustery day. Enjoy the naturally nutty taste of brown rice with fresh mushrooms in *Beef and Brown Rice Casserole*. If a more delicate flavor is your preference, *Canadian Bacon, Asparagus, and Potato Frittata* is a mouth-watering dish to savor.

Entice appetites at a special luncheon with *Speedy Spinach and Chicken Sausage Lasagna* or *Fettuccine with Portabella Mushrooms, Ham, and Cream*. These sensational recipes are both a treat for the eyes as well as the palate.

Turn up the heat with *Chicken Enchiladas, Fire Fighter's Chili* and the southern favorite *Bayou Jambalaya*, a jazzy blend of rice, sausage, ham, and shrimp. Relish the spicy fragrance of apple juice-simmered sauerkraut and sausages in *Pork and Kraut Casserole*.

The recipes in this chapter will please the cook as well as a wide range of appetites. Best of all, to round out these meals, all you'll need is perhaps a tossed salad and a simple dessert. Bon appétit!

Fire Fighter's Chili

8	ounces mild or hot Italian sausage, casing removed, crumbled		½	teaspoon beef flavor instant bouillon
8	ounces lean ground beef		⅓	cup Worcestershire sauce
⅓	cup chopped onion		2 to 3	tablespoons chili powder
2	cloves garlic, minced		1	tablespoon honey
2	14½-ounce cans diced tomatoes		¼	teaspoon crushed red pepper
1	15-ounce can kidney or pinto beans, drained, rinsed		¼	teaspoon celery seed
½	cup dry red wine		¼	teaspoon hot pepper sauce
½	cup water			Salt and pepper

Cook sausage and ground beef in skillet at 350° until brown. Remove from skillet. Pour off excess drippings, reserving 1 tablespoon in skillet. Add onion and garlic; cook 1 minute. Stir in meats and remaining ingredients, except salt and pepper; heat at 400° until boiling. Reduce heat to simmer, between Warm and 200°; cook, covered, 30 minutes, stirring occasionally. Season to taste with salt and pepper.

4 servings

Bayou Jambalaya

1	tablespoon vegetable oil		½	teaspoon dried thyme leaves
½	cup chopped onion		¼	teaspoon cayenne pepper
1	green pepper, chopped		⅛	teaspoon ground cloves
1	clove garlic, minced		⅛	teaspoon ground nutmeg
1	tablespoon flour		3 to 4	drops hot pepper sauce
8	ounces pork link sausages, cut into 1-inch pieces		½	teaspoon salt
8	ounces baked ham, cubed		3	cups cooked rice
1	14½-ounce can diced tomatoes		8	ounces uncooked shrimp, peeled, deveined
1	cup water			Minced parsley
1	teaspoon chicken flavor instant bouillon			

Heat oil in skillet at 225°. Add onion, green pepper, and garlic; cook until tender. Stir in flour; cook 1 minute. Stir in sausage and ham; cook at 300° until sausage is brown and no longer pink in the center, 7 to 8 minutes, stirring occasionally. Stir in tomatoes, water, bouillon, thyme, cayenne pepper, cloves, nutmeg, hot pepper sauce, and salt; cook at 400° until boiling. Reduce heat to simmer, between Warm and 200°; cook, covered, 15 minutes. Stir in rice and shrimp; cook, uncovered, until shrimp is pink, 3 to 4 minutes, stirring occasionally. Serve in bowls; sprinkle with parsley.

4 to 6 servings

Beef Vegetable Stew with Dill Dumplings

3	tablespoons vegetable oil	⅔	cup tomato sauce
1½	pounds beef cubes	1	bay leaf
1	cup chopped onion	½	teaspoon curry powder
1	clove garlic, minced	3	large carrots, cut diagonally into
3	tablespoons all-purpose flour		1½-inch pieces
3	cups water	4	ounces mushrooms, quartered
1½	teaspoons beef flavor	1	cup frozen peas
	instant bouillon		**Dill Dumplings** (see recipe below)

Heat skillet at 350°. Add oil and beef; cook until brown, about 8 minutes. Remove beef. Pour off excess drippings, reserving 1 tablespoon in skillet. Add onion and garlic; cook at 225° until onion is tender. Stir in flour; cook 2 minutes. Stir in water, bouillon, tomato sauce, bay leaf, and curry powder; heat at 400° until boiling. Reduce heat to simmer, between Warm and 200°. Add meat; cook, covered, until meat is tender, about 1½ hours. Add carrots during last 30 minutes of cooking time. Stir in mushrooms and peas.

Make Dill Dumplings. Drop dough by tablespoons onto stew; cook, uncovered, 10 minutes. Cook, covered, until dumplings are puffed and cooked through, 10 to 12 minutes.

6 servings

Dill Dumplings

1½	cups buttermilk baking mix
½	cup milk
1½	teaspoons dried dillweed

Combine all ingredients in small bowl; stir until just mixed.

6 servings

Three-Meat Stew

3	tablespoons vegetable oil	2	tablespoons paprika
8	ounces beef cubes	2	cups water
8	ounces veal cubes	1	teaspoon beef flavor instant bouillon
8	ounces pork cubes	1	14½-ounce can diced tomatoes
1	cup chopped onion	⅔	cup tomato sauce
1	cup chopped green pepper	¼	teaspoon caraway seed, crushed
1	clove garlic, minced	1	bay leaf
1	cup sliced mushrooms		Salt and pepper
¼	cup all-purpose flour		

Heat skillet at 350°. Add oil and meats; cook until brown, about 8 minutes. Remove meats. Pour off excess drippings, reserving 1 tablespoon in skillet. Add onions, green pepper, and garlic; cook at 225° for 5 minutes. Stir in mushrooms; cook 2 minutes. Stir in flour and paprika; cook 1 minute. Stir in meats, water, bouillon, tomatoes, tomato sauce, caraway seed, and bay leaf; heat at 400° until boiling. Reduce heat to simmer, between Warm and 200°; cook, covered, until meats are tender, 1½ to 1¾ hours, stirring occasionally. Season to taste with salt and pepper.

6 servings

Fiesta Taco Salad

4	cups coarsely chopped iceberg lettuce	2	tablespoons chopped tomato
2	cups romaine lettuce, torn into bite-size pieces	1½	teaspoons chili powder
1	tablespoon vegetable oil	¼	teaspoon salt
1	onion, chopped	¼	teaspoon ground cumin
1	clove garlic, minced	⅛	teaspoon cayenne pepper
8	ounces lean ground beef	1	small avocado, peeled, pitted, chopped
¼	cup tomato sauce	½	cup shredded Monterey Jack or cheddar cheese
2	tablespoons chopped red or green pepper		Tortilla chips, crushed

Toss greens in salad bowl.

Heat skillet at 250°. Add oil, onion, and garlic; cook 1 to 2 minutes. Add ground beef; cook at 350° until browned, stirring occasionally. Pour excess drippings from skillet. Stir in tomato sauce, pepper, tomato, chili powder, salt, cumin, and cayenne pepper; cook until mixture is hot and beginning to thicken, about 3 minutes, stirring constantly. Spoon hot beef mixture over greens and toss. Spoon salad onto serving plates; sprinkle with avocado, cheese, and tortilla chips.

4 servings

Irish Lamb Stew

2	tablespoons vegetable oil		1	teaspoon minced parsley
1½	pounds lamb cubes		¼	teaspoon dried thyme leaves
2	medium onions, sliced		1	bay leaf
3	tablespoons all-purpose flour		4	small potatoes, peeled, cut into fourths
2	cups water			
1½	teaspoons chicken flavor instant bouillon		4	medium carrots, cut into ½-inch slices
1½	teaspoons Worcestershire sauce			Salt and pepper

Heat skillet at 350°. Add oil and lamb; cook until brown. Remove lamb. Add onions; cook at 225° until tender. Stir in flour; cook 2 minutes. Add lamb, water, bouillon, Worcestershire, parsley, thyme, and bay leaf; cook at 400° until boiling. Reduce heat to simmer, between Warm and 200°; cook, covered, until lamb is tender, 1¼ to 1½ hours. Add potatoes and carrots during last 30 minutes of cooking time. Season to taste with salt and pepper.

4 servings

Deep-Pan Pizza

1	16-ounce package hot roll mix			Olive oil
1¼	cups warm water (120° to 130°)			Cornmeal
3	tablespoons olive oil, divided		1	cup pizza sauce
1	cup sliced mushrooms		1 to 2	ounces sliced pepperoni
1	cup sliced green pepper		1	cup shredded mozzarella cheese
½	cup chopped onion		1	cup shredded cheddar cheese

Follow the "pizza recipe" directions on the package of the hot roll mix for mixing and kneading dough, increasing the water to 1¼ cups, adding 2 tablespoons oil, and omitting the eggs.

Heat skillet at 225°. Add remaining 1 tablespoon oil, mushrooms, pepper, and onion; cook until onion is tender. Remove vegetable mixture from skillet; reserve. Clean skillet.

Grease bottom of skillet lightly with oil; sprinkle lightly with cornmeal. Pat dough out evenly in bottom of skillet; cook, covered, at 200° for 20 minutes. Lightly brush top of dough with oil and sprinkle lightly with cornmeal. Carefully turn dough over in skillet. Increase temperature to 250°. Spoon sauce evenly on crust. Top with reserved vegetable mixture. Arrange pepperoni over vegetable mixture. Sprinkle cheese over all; cook, covered, until cooked through, 20 minutes. Cut into squares with plastic or wooden utensil.

4 to 6 servings

Beef and Brown Rice Casserole

2 tablespoons vegetable oil	¼ teaspoon dried chervil leaves
1 pound lean beef top round steak, cut into ¾-inch pieces	1½ cups brown rice
1 cup sliced mushrooms	4 cups water
½ cup thinly sliced celery	1 teaspoon beef flavor instant bouillon
2 green onions, sliced	1 cup sour cream
1 teaspoon minced parsley	Salt and pepper
½ teaspoon dried savory leaves	

Heat skillet at 350°. Add oil and beef; cook until browned on all sides, about 5 minutes. Stir in mushrooms, celery, onions, parsley, savory, and chervil; cook at 225° until vegetables are tender, about 4 minutes, stirring occasionally. Stir in rice; cook 2 minutes, stirring occasionally. Stir in water and bouillon; cook at 400° until boiling. Reduce heat to simmer, between Warm and 200°; cook, covered, until rice is tender and liquid absorbed, 55 to 60 minutes, stirring occasionally, adding more water if necessary. Reduce heat to Warm. Stir in sour cream; season to taste with salt and pepper.

4 servings

Pork and Kraut Casserole

1 tablespoon vegetable oil	4 potatoes, peeled, cut into halves
4 pork chops, ¾ inch thick	1½ cups apple juice
4 fully cooked Polish sausages (about 8 ounces)	2 tablespoons cider vinegar
1 large onion, sliced	1 tablespoon light brown sugar
2 14-ounce cans sauerkraut, drained	4 whole cloves
	¼ teaspoon ground nutmeg
	Salt and pepper

Heat skillet at 350°. Add oil, pork chops, and sausages; cook until well browned, about 3 minutes on each side. Remove meats. Add onion; cook at 225° for 2 minutes. Add pork chops, sauerkraut, potatoes, apple juice, vinegar, sugar, cloves, and nutmeg; cook at 400° until boiling. Reduce heat to simmer, between Warm and 200°; cook, covered, until pork chops are tender, 25 to 30 minutes. Add sausages to skillet during last 15 minutes of cooking time. Season to taste with salt and pepper.

4 to 6 servings

Pork Chop and Sweet Potato Casserole

4 to 6	pork loin chops, ½ inch thick		3	tablespoons dark molasses
	Poultry seasoning		1	tablespoon lemon juice
	Salt and pepper		¼	cup light brown sugar
1	tablespoon vegetable oil		¼	teaspoon anise seed, crushed
1	15-ounce can sliced peaches, drained, juice reserved		1	17-ounce can sweet potatoes, drained

Sprinkle chops lightly with poultry seasoning, salt, and pepper. Heat skillet at 350°. Add oil and chops; cook until browned on both sides. Stir in reserved juice, molasses, lemon juice, brown sugar, and anise seed; cook at 400° until boiling. Reduce heat to simmer, between Warm and 200°; cook, covered, 20 minutes. Add sweet potatoes and peaches, spooning sauce over; cook, covered, 10 minutes, or until pork chops are fork-tender.

4 to 6 servings

Canadian Bacon, Asparagus, and Potato Frittata

8	large eggs, beaten			Salt
1	cup shredded Gouda cheese, divided		1½	cups slivered yellow onions
½	teaspoon salt		1	5- to 6-ounce package sliced Canadian bacon, cut into ½-inch pieces
⅛	teaspoon pepper			
2	tablespoons olive oil, divided		12	asparagus spears, cut diagonally into 1-inch pieces
2	cups new red potatoes, sliced ⅛ inch thick (about 8 potatoes)			

Whisk eggs, ½ cup cheese, salt, and pepper in medium bowl. Reserve.

Heat skillet at 350°. Add 1 tablespoon oil and potatoes; sprinkle potatoes lightly with salt. Cook until potatoes are tender and browned, about 10 minutes, turning occasionally. Remove potatoes as they are done to a small bowl. Reserve.

Add remaining 1 tablespoon oil and onions to skillet; cook, until tender and light browned, about 5 minutes, stirring frequently. Add Canadian bacon and asparagus; cook until asparagus is bright green and crisp-tender, about 5 minutes, stirring occasionally. Stir in reserved potatoes. Stir in reserved egg mixture distributing evenly with vegetables. As soon as some of the eggs begin to set, smooth the surface; sprinkle remaining ½ cup cheese on top. Cook, covered, until eggs are almost set, about 7 to 9 minutes. Turn heat off. Let stand until eggs are completely set, about 3 to 5 minutes. Cut into squares with plastic or wooden utensil.

Preparation Tip: *To make onion slivers, cut onion in half crosswise, then into thin wedges.*

6 to 8 servings

Almond Chicken Casserole

4	boneless skinless chicken breast halves (about 1¼ pounds)		1	teaspoon minced parsley
1	tablespoon butter or margarine		¼	teaspoon dried thyme leaves
2	tablespoons vegetable oil		2	cups water
1	cup chopped onion		1½	teaspoons chicken flavor instant bouillon
1	cup sliced mushrooms		½	cup frozen peas, thawed
½	cup chopped green pepper		6	ounces egg noodles, cooked, drained
¼	cup sliced carrot		½	cup slivered almonds, toasted
¼	cup sliced celery		¼	teaspoon cayenne pepper
1	clove garlic, minced			Salt and pepper
¼	cup all-purpose flour			

Cut chicken into ½-inch pieces. Heat butter and oil in skillet at Warm until butter is melted. Add chicken; cook at 350° until chicken is no longer pink in the center, about 5 minutes. Remove chicken and reserve. Stir in onion, mushrooms, green pepper, carrot, celery, and garlic; cook 3 minutes, stirring frequently. Stir in flour, parsley, and thyme; cook 2 minutes, stirring constantly. Stir in water and bouillon; cook at 400° until boiling. Reduce heat to simmer, between Warm and 200°; cook, covered, 5 minutes; uncovered, 3 minutes. Stir in reserved chicken and peas; cook 2 minutes. Stir in noodles and almonds; cook until heated through, about 5 minutes. Stir in cayenne pepper; season to taste with salt and pepper.

4 servings

Chicken and Artichoke Casserole

6	boneless skinless chicken breast halves (about 2 pounds)		¼	teaspoon dried tarragon leaves
	All-purpose flour		⅛	teaspoon dried marjoram leaves
2	tablespoons vegetable oil		1	9-ounce package frozen artichoke hearts
	Salt and pepper		2	tomatoes, cut into wedges
1	cup water		1	medium onion, sliced
½	teaspoon chicken flavor instant bouillon		1	medium green pepper, sliced
¼	cup dry sherry		1	cup mushrooms, cut into halves
¼	teaspoon dried rosemary leaves			Hot cooked rice

Coat chicken lightly with flour. Heat skillet at 350°. Add oil and chicken; cook, covered, until golden, about 5 minutes on each side. Sprinkle chicken lightly with salt and pepper. Add water, bouillon, sherry, rosemary, tarragon, and marjoram; heat at 400° until boiling. Reduce heat to simmer, between Warm and 200°; cook, covered, 15 minutes. Add artichoke hearts, tomatoes, onion, and green pepper; cook, covered, until artichokes are tender, about 10 minutes. Stir in mushrooms; cook, covered, 5 minutes. Serve with rice.

6 servings

Chicken and Pork Fried Rice

2	tablespoons vegetable oil	¼	cup chopped celery
4	cups cooked rice	4	shiitake mushrooms, coarsely chopped
1	cup coarsely chopped cooked chicken	3	eggs, beaten
¾	cup coarsely chopped cooked pork	3	tablespoons soy sauce
½	cup thinly sliced green onions, divided	1	teaspoon sugar
		¼	teaspoon ground ginger

Heat skillet at 250°. Add oil and rice; cook until heated through, 6 to 8 minutes, stirring occasionally. Stir in chicken, pork, ⅓ cup onions, celery, and mushrooms; cook until heated through, 3 to 5 minutes. Mix eggs, soy sauce, sugar, and ginger in small bowl. Add to rice mixture; cook until eggs are set, stirring occasionally. Serve with remaining onions.

4 servings

Chicken Enchiladas

1	15-ounce can tomato sauce	½	cup chopped onion
½	cup water	1	4-ounce can chopped green chiles
2	tablespoons distilled white vinegar	1	clove garlic, minced
1	tablespoon sugar	12	5- to 6-inch corn tortillas
2	teaspoons chili powder	2	cups shredded cheddar or Monterey Jack cheese
1	teaspoon salt		Sliced black olives
1	teaspoon paprika		Chopped avocado
½	teaspoon dried oregano leaves		Sour cream
¼	teaspoon ground cumin		
¼	teaspoon cayenne pepper		
2	cups shredded cooked chicken		

Mix tomato sauce, water, vinegar, sugar, chili powder, salt, paprika, oregano, cumin, and cayenne pepper in skillet; cook at 400° until boiling. Turn heat to Off.

Combine chicken, onion, chiles, and garlic in medium bowl; stir in 1 cup of the sauce from skillet. Dip 1 tortilla in sauce in skillet to soften. Spoon about 2 tablespoons of the chicken mixture and 2 tablespoons cheese on tortilla; roll up. Repeat with remaining tortillas.

Arrange tortillas, seam sides down, in sauce in skillet; heat at 400° until boiling. Reduce heat to Warm. Sprinkle remaining cheese over tortillas; cook, covered, at Warm until tortillas are heated, about 15 minutes. Sprinkle with olives and avocado; serve with sour cream, as desired.

6 servings

Bow-Tie Tuna Casserole

3 tablespoons unsalted butter, divided	2 teaspoons Dijon-style mustard
¼ cup dry breadcrumbs	½ cup sliced green onions
¼ cup grated Parmesan cheese	½ cup frozen peas, thawed
2 tablespoons all-purpose flour	2 tablespoons chopped flat-leaf parsley
¼ teaspoon salt	1 tablespoon fresh lemon juice
1½ cups milk	2 teaspoons dried marjoram
2 6-ounce cans tuna, packed in water, drained	1 teaspoon grated lemon peel, optional
8 ounces bow-tie pasta, cooked, drained	Salt and pepper

Heat 1 tablespoon butter in skillet at Warm until melted and foamy. Add breadcrumbs; heat at 225° until golden, stirring occasionally. Remove to small bowl; when cool mix in Parmesan cheese. Reserve.

Heat remaining 2 tablespoons butter in skillet at Warm until melted. Blend in flour and salt. Cook for 1 minute. Add milk; cook at 250° until sauce thickens and bubbles, stirring constantly. Reduce heat to Warm. Stir in tuna, pasta, mustard, onions, peas, parsley, lemon juice, marjoram, and lemon peel. Cook until heated through, 5 to 8 minutes, stirring occasionally. Season to taste with salt and pepper. Sprinkle with breadcrumb mixture.

6 servings

Speedy Spinach and Chicken Sausage Lasagna

1 15-ounce container part-skim ricotta cheese	9 oven-ready lasagna noodles
1 egg, beaten	2 cups baby spinach leaves (2 ounces)
¼ cup plus 2 tablespoons prepared pesto, divided	2 fully cooked chicken or turkey Italian sausages (6 to 8 ounces total), diced
1 26-ounce jar Italian baking or marinara sauce	2 cups shredded mozzarella cheese
	¼ cup shredded Parmesan cheese

Mix ricotta cheese, egg, and ¼ cup pesto in small bowl. Reserve.

Spread ½ cup sauce on bottom of skillet. Lay three noodles over sauce, breaking as necessary to cover skillet. Top noodles with half of the ricotta cheese mixture, 1 cup spinach, half of the sausage, 1 cup sauce, and 1 cup mozzarella. Repeat layering, omitting mozzarella cheese. Finish layering with the last three noodles, remaining sauce, remaining 2 tablespoons pesto, 1 cup mozzarella cheese, and all the Parmesan cheese. Cover skillet. Cook at 200° until noodles are tender and lasagna is hot, about 45 to 50 minutes.

6 to 8 servings

Spaghetti with Chicken Cutlets and Marinara Sauce

Marinara Sauce (see recipe below)
- ½ cup all-purpose flour
- ½ teaspoon salt
- ¼ teaspoon pepper
- 6 boneless skinless chicken breast halves (about 2 pounds)

- 3 tablespoons olive oil
- 1 pound spaghetti, cooked, drained
  Grated Parmesan cheese

Make Marinara Sauce; remove to bowl. Clean skillet.

Combine flour, salt, and pepper in small bowl. Pound chicken to ½ thickness. Coat chicken lightly with seasoned flour mixture. Heat skillet at 350°. Add oil and chicken; cook until brown, 3 to 4 minutes on each side. Remove chicken and keep warm. Add spaghetti; cook at 225° for 1 minute. Stir in Marinara Sauce. Arrange chicken on spaghetti mixture. Sprinkle generously with cheese; cook, covered, until heated through, about 2 minutes.

4 to 6 servings

Marinara Sauce

- 2 tablespoons olive oil
- 1½ cups minced onions
- 1 cup finely chopped carrots
- ½ cup chopped green pepper
- 2 cloves garlic, minced
- 2 14½-ounce cans diced Italian plum tomatoes
- 3 tablespoons tomato paste
- 1 cup water
- 2 teaspoons light brown sugar

- 1 teaspoon dried basil leaves
- ½ teaspoon chicken flavor instant bouillon
- ½ teaspoon dried oregano leaves
- 1 bay leaf
- ½ teaspoon salt
- ¼ teaspoon pepper
- ¼ teaspoon fennel seeds, crushed
- 2 tablespoons grated Parmesan cheese

Heat skillet at 225°. Add oil, onions, carrots, green pepper, and garlic; cook 5 minutes, stirring frequently. Stir in remaining ingredients, except Parmesan cheese; cook at 400° until boiling. Reduce heat to simmer between Warm and 200°; cook, covered, 1¼ hours. Stir in cheese.

About 4 cups

Spaghetti Carbonara

1½	tablespoons olive oil
½	cup coarsely chopped baked ham
1	clove garlic, minced
¼	cup frozen peas, thawed
8	ounces spaghetti, cooked, drained

2	eggs, beaten
¼	cup grated Parmesan cheese
¼	teaspoon salt
⅛	teaspoon cayenne pepper

Heat skillet at 300°. Add oil, ham, and garlic; cook 2 minutes. Stir in peas and spaghetti; cook until heated through, 3 to 4 minutes, stirring occasionally. Whisk eggs, cheese, salt, and cayenne pepper in small bowl; pour egg mixture over spaghetti. Turn heat to Warm; toss spaghetti until egg mixture is set, 2 to 3 minutes.

2 servings

Fettuccine with Portabella Mushrooms, Ham, and Cream

3	tablespoons butter, divided
8	ounces maple glazed ham, cut into ¼-inch dice
½	cup chopped walnuts
8	ounces baby portabella mushrooms, cut into ¼-inch slices
2	teaspoons minced garlic

¼	cup white wine
¾	cup heavy cream
½	cup grated Parmesan cheese, plus additional for serving
	Salt and pepper
8	ounces fettuccine, cooked, drained
¼	cup finely chopped parsley

Heat 1 tablespoon butter in skillet at 225°. Add ham and walnuts; cook until walnuts are toasted, about 4 to 5 minutes, stirring frequently. Remove and reserve.

Melt remaining 2 tablespoons butter in skillet. Increase temperature to 325°. Add mushrooms and garlic; cook until mushrooms start to brown and just begin to give off liquid, about 3 minutes, stirring frequently. Add wine; cook until most of the liquid has evaporated, about 2 minutes. Add cream, reduce heat to 250°; cook until slightly thickened, about 2 minutes. Reduce heat to Warm and stir in cheese. Season to taste with salt and pepper. Stir in fettuccine; toss to coat. Add reserved ham, walnuts and parsley; toss to combine. Cook until heated through. Serve with additional Parmesan, as desired.

4 servings

Sandwiches

Let the inspiring recipes in this chapter transform your kitchen into everyone's favorite deli. Whether you're looking for a loaded sandwich with big flavor or a quick lunch for the less-than-hearty appetite, you will be sure to find it here.

The *Philly Beef Sandwiches*, *Shrimp Rolls*, and *Pesto Chicken Sandwiches* are right on target when time is tight. However, explore the *Texas-Style Beef Barbecue* when you're home for the afternoon and have time to let it simmer to perfection…it's definitely worth the wait.

Time-honored favorites like *Pastrami Reubens* and *Canadian Bacon Grill* are ideal for carefree weekend meals or football parties. When your routine collection of recipes no longer sparks any interest, recharge your menu with the lively *Teriyaki Steak Wraps*, *Mediterranean Chicken Wraps*, or *Lemon Chicken Pitas with Garlic Yogurt Sauce*. They are simple to prepare and will please the whole gang.

The electric skillet is a fantastic grill to have on hand. Its nonstick surface and easily regulated temperature make it the perfect candidate for the "deli" craving in all of us. Whatever recipe you choose, you'll be delighted with the results and so will your "diners."

Texas-Style Beef Barbecue

2	tablespoons vegetable oil		3	tablespoons cider vinegar
3	pounds beef cubes for stew		1	tablespoon Worcestershire sauce
1	cup chopped onion		⅓	cup light brown sugar
2	cups water		2	teaspoons dry mustard
2	teaspoons beef flavor instant bouillon		1	teaspoon ground allspice
1	cup chili sauce		½	teaspoon salt
1	cup ketchup		½	teaspoon pepper
			8	hamburger buns, toasted

Heat skillet at 350°. Add oil, beef cubes, and onion; cook until beef is brown and onion is tender, about 5 minutes. Add water and bouillon; cook at 400° until boiling. Reduce heat to simmer between Warm and 200°; cook, covered, until beef is tender, about 2 hours. Shred beef in skillet using a fork to pull meat apart. Stir in remaining ingredients, except buns; cook at 400° until boiling. Reduce heat to simmer between Warm and 200°; cook, covered, 15 minutes, stirring occasionally. Serve hot beef mixture on toasted buns.

8 servings

Philly Beef Sandwiches

4	hoagie or small French rolls, cut in half		½	teaspoon beef flavor instant bouillon
	Butter or margarine, softened		¼	teaspoon dried basil leaves
1	tablespoon vegetable oil		⅛	teaspoon pepper
1	medium onion, sliced		8	ounces thinly sliced medium-rare roast beef
1	medium green pepper, cut into thin strips		4	1-ounce slices American cheese, cut diagonally into halves
½	cup water			

Spread cut sides of rolls lightly with butter. Heat skillet at 275°. Place rolls, cut sides down, in skillet; cook until toasted. Remove rolls.

Reduce heat to 225°. Add oil, onion, and green pepper; cook until tender, about 5 minutes. Stir in water, bouillon, basil, and pepper; cook 2 minutes. Stir in beef; cook until heated, 2 to 3 minutes.

Place ½ cheese slice on bottom half of each roll. Top each with beef mixture, ½ cheese slice, and top half of roll. Clean skillet. Place sandwiches on rack in skillet; cook, covered, at 350° until cheese is melted, 4 to 5 minutes.

4 servings

Steak Sandwiches with Blue Cheese

4	slices Italian bread, ¾ inch thick		1	teaspoon dried chives
	Butter or margarine, softened		½	teaspoon Bavarian-style mustard
1	tablespoon vegetable oil		¼	teaspoon prepared horseradish
4	cube or minute steaks		2	tablespoons crumbled blue cheese

Spread bread slices lightly with softened butter. Heat skillet at 275°. Place bread, buttered sides down, in skillet; cook until toasted. Remove bread. Add oil and steaks to skillet; cook at 350° to desired degree of doneness. Place steaks on toasted bread. Stir chives, mustard, and horseradish into skillet; cook 2 minutes. Stir in blue cheese until it begins to melt; serve sauce over steaks.

4 servings

Canadian Bacon Grill

4	hoagie or small French rolls, cut in half		2	tablespoons butter or margarine
	Butter or margarine, softened		2	teaspoons dried chives
½	teaspoon garlic powder		¼	teaspoon prepared horseradish
¼	teaspoon dried thyme leaves		8	ounces sliced Canadian bacon

Spread cut sides of rolls lightly with butter. Mix garlic powder and thyme in small bowl; sprinkle evenly over butter. Heat skillet at 275°. Place rolls, cut sides down, in skillet; cook until toasted. Remove rolls. Heat butter in skillet at Warm until melted. Stir in chives, horseradish, and Canadian bacon; cook, covered, at 300° for 2 minutes. Serve Canadian bacon mixture on toasted rolls.

4 servings

Triple Cheese Grill

2	tablespoons mayonnaise		2	1-ounce slices brick or Monterey Jack cheese
⅛	teaspoon dried basil leaves			
⅛	teaspoon dried oregano leaves		2	thin slices tomato
4	slices whole wheat bread		2	1-ounce slices provolone cheese
2	1-ounce slices cheddar cheese			Softened butter or margarine

Mix mayonnaise, basil, and oregano in small bowl; spread mixture on one side of each bread slice. Top 2 slices of bread with 1 slice each of cheddar cheese, brick cheese, tomato, provolone cheese, and bread slice. Lightly butter bread on outside of sandwiches. Heat skillet at 275°. Add sandwiches, cook until golden on bottom. Flip sandwiches over; cook until bread is golden and cheese is melted.

2 servings

Pastrami Reubens

¼	cup mayonnaise	12	ounces sliced pastrami
1	teaspoon spicy brown mustard	1	14-ounce can sauerkraut, drained
¼	teaspoon caraway seed	4	1-ounce slices Monterey Jack cheese
8	slices rye bread	2	tablespoons butter or margarine

Mix mayonnaise, mustard, and caraway seed in small bowl; spread on one side of 4 bread slices. Top with pastrami, sauerkraut, and cheese, equally divided between bread slices. Top with remaining bread. Heat butter in skillet at Warm until butter is melted. Add sandwiches; cook, covered at 275° until heated through, about 3 minutes on each side.

4 servings

Italian Sausage with Pepperonata

1 to 1¼	pounds mild or hot Italian sausage, cut into 5-inch pieces	2	medium red peppers, sliced
¼	cup butter or margarine		Water
1	large red onion, sliced		Salt and pepper
2	medium green peppers, sliced	4	hoagie or French rolls, cut in half lengthwise

Cook sausage in skillet at 325° until browned and no longer pink in the center, about 10 minutes. Remove sausage; reserve.

Heat butter in skillet at Warm until melted. Add onion; cook at 225° until onion is golden, about 10 minutes, stirring occasionally. Add green and red peppers; cook, covered, until very soft, about 20 minutes, adding water, ¼ cup at a time if mixture becomes too dry. Add reserved sausage; cook, covered, until heated through, 2 to 3 minutes. Season to taste with salt and pepper. Serve sausage and pepper mixture in rolls.

4 servings

Pizza Bread

1	10-inch loaf French bread	½	cup chopped green pepper
	Olive oil	½	cup tomato sauce
1	tablespoon olive oil	1¼	teaspoons dried basil leaves
1	cup chopped onion	1	teaspoon dried oregano leaves
1	cup sliced mushrooms	1	cup shredded mozzarella cheese

Cut bread lengthwise in half; brush cut sides of bread lightly with olive oil. Heat skillet at 275°. Place bread, cut sides down, in skillet; cook until toasted. Remove bread.

Heat oil in skillet at 225°. Add onion, mushrooms, and pepper; cook until onion is tender, about 5 minutes. Remove onion mixture; reserve. Clean skillet.

Mix tomato sauce, basil, and oregano in small bowl; spread on toasted side of bread halves. Top with vegetable mixture; sprinkle with cheese. Place bread on rack in skillet; cook, covered, at 300° until cheese is melted, about 5 minutes.

6 servings

Shrimp Rolls

1	loaf Italian bread, cut into 1½-inch slices	¼	teaspoon cayenne pepper
	Butter or margarine, softened	1	pound cooked shrimp, peeled, deveined, chopped
½	cup mayonnaise	½	cup finely chopped celery
1	teaspoon Dijon-style mustard	2	tablespoons thinly sliced green onions
1	teaspoon lemon juice		

Cut bread slices again vertically to form rolls, slicing to, but not through, bottom of bread. Spread outsides of rolls lightly with butter. Heat skillet at 275°. Add rolls; cook until toasted on both sides. Remove rolls.

Combine mayonnaise, mustard, lemon juice, and pepper in medium bowl. Mix in shrimp, celery, and onion. Serve shrimp mixture in toasted buns.

4 servings

Pesto Chicken Sandwiches

4	boneless skinless chicken breast halves (about 1¼ pounds)		8	thin slices tomato
1	tablespoon olive oil		8	½-ounce slices provolone cheese
½	cup prepared pesto sauce		3	tablespoons butter, melted
8	slices crusty sour dough bread, ¼ inch thick			

Pound chicken breasts lightly until even in thickness. Heat skillet at 350°. Add oil and chicken; cook until chicken is cooked through, about 4 to 5 minutes per side. Remove from skillet; cool completely. Slice chicken into ¼-inch strips.

Spread 1 tablespoon pesto on one side of each bread slice. Divide chicken evenly between 4 of the slices. Place 2 slices each of tomato and cheese over chicken. Cover with remaining bread slices, pesto side facing cheese.

Brush outside of each sandwich with melted butter. Heat skillet at 325°. Toast sandwiches until bread is golden and cheese is melted, about 2 to 3 minutes per side.

Preparation Tip: Chicken may be cooked in advance and refrigerated until needed.

4 servings

Mediterranean Chicken Wraps

4	boneless skinless chicken breast halves, cut into ¼-inch strips (about 1¼ pounds)		1	cup green pepper strips
			4	flour tortillas (8-inch diameter)
½	cup bottled Italian dressing		½	cup crumbled feta cheese
1	cup thinly sliced onion		¼	cup chopped kalamata olives

Place chicken in shallow glass baking dish. Pour dressing over chicken. Refrigerate, covered, 30 minutes to 1 hour, turning occasionally.

Heat skillet at 325°. Remove chicken from marinade; discard marinade. Add chicken, onion, and pepper to skillet. Stir-fry until chicken is cooked through, 5 to 6 minutes. Divide chicken mixture evenly between tortillas. Top each with cheese and olives; roll tightly.

4 servings

Lemon Chicken Pitas with Garlic Yogurt Sauce

Garlic Yogurt Sauce (see recipe below)
1¼ pound boneless skinless chicken breast halves
2 tablespoons fresh lemon juice
2 tablespoons olive oil
1 tablespoon minced fresh oregano or 1 teaspoon dried
1 teaspoon finely grated lemon peel
½ teaspoon salt
¼ teaspoon pepper
4 pita rounds, heated
16 tomato slices (about 2 tomatoes)
24 thin cucumber slices, peeled or unpeeled as desired

Make Garlic Yogurt Sauce; reserve.

Pound chicken breasts lightly to ½-inch thickness. Place chicken in shallow glass baking dish. Combine lemon juice, oil, oregano, lemon peel, salt, and pepper in small bowl. Pour over chicken; refrigerate, covered, 30 minutes to 2 hours.

Heat skillet at 325°. Remove chicken from marinade; discard marinade. Add chicken to skillet; cook until it springs back when touched, about 9 to 11 minutes, turning every 3 minutes. Allow chicken to cool, cut into slices.

Cut each pita round in half. Fill equally with chicken, tomato, and cucumber. Drizzle Garlic Yogurt Sauce equally in each pita.

8 servings

Garlic Yogurt Sauce

1 6-ounce container plain nonfat or lowfat yogurt, drained of liquid
2 tablespoons crumbled feta cheese
1 teaspoon minced garlic
1 teaspoon lemon juice
¼ teaspoon salt
⅛ teaspoon pepper

Mix all ingredients in small bowl. Cover and refrigerate until ready to serve.

Greek-Style Pitas

1	pound top sirloin steak about ½-inch thick, cut into ¼-inch strips	2	pita rounds, cut into halves	
½	cup bottled Greek vinaigrette dressing	¼	cup seeded chopped cucumber	
2	large cloves garlic, minced	¼	cup julienned sun-dried tomatoes packed in oil, drained	
1	tablespoon chopped fresh oregano or 1 teaspoon dried oregano	¼	cup chopped onion	
1½	teaspoons grated lemon peel	2	tablespoons chopped kalamata or black olives	
		¼	cup plain yogurt	

Place steak in shallow glass baking dish. Pour dressing over steak. Cover and refrigerate 1 to 2 hours.

Heat skillet at 350°. Add steak and dressing, garlic, oregano, and lemon peel to skillet. Heat until steak is cooked through, about 4 to 5 minutes.

Divide steak, half of sauce, cucumber, tomatoes, onion, and olives evenly between pita halves. Top each pita half with 1 tablespoon yogurt.

Substitution Tip: Bottled Italian dressing may be substituted for Greek vinaigrette dressing.

4 servings

Teriyaki Steak Wraps

½	cup teriyaki sauce	1	pound top sirloin steak, ½-inch thick, cut into ¼-inch strips	
2	teaspoons lime juice	1	cup red pepper strips	
2	teaspoons sesame oil	1	cup shredded carrot	
2	teaspoons sugar	½	cup shredded green cabbage	
¼	teaspoon crushed red pepper	4	flour tortillas (10-inch diameter)	

Combine teriyaki sauce, lime juice, sesame oil, sugar, and red pepper in shallow glass baking dish. Stir in beef strips. Refrigerate, covered, 1 to 2 hours.

Heat skillet at 350°. Remove beef from marinade; discard marinade. Add beef to skillet; fry until cooked though, about 5 minutes. Add vegetables during last minute of cooking.

Divide mixture evenly between tortillas. Roll up tightly.

4 servings

Desserts

Although the electric skillet doesn't seem a likely vessel for making desserts, this chapter's impressive recipes will make you rethink how to prepare desserts and candy in the future. There's something for everyone…charming summer-fresh fruit desserts, creamy custards, dreamy cakes, tempting chocolate desserts, and magnificent melt-in-your-mouth candies.

These hard to resist desserts come in all styles, and there is a time and place for each of them. Strawberries' short season make them the precious nectar of summer. So, be sure to take the time to enjoy the brightly flavored *Fresh Strawberry Tart*. It truly is remarkable! For a comfy, home-for-the-day kind of dessert, try *Cranberry Pecan Bread Pudding* or *Fruit and Nut Filled Apples*. Memories from your childhood will come pouring out of every gratifying bite.

Sour Cream Rhubarb Cake is a delightful dessert…not too sweet, not too tart…and ideal for a visit with friends. The scrumptious *Chocolate Raspberry Pudding Cake* provides an element of surprise with its warm chocolatey molten inside. If elegance is the theme, *Chocolate Fudge Cheesecake* is the ticket, as well as the simple, yet well-dressed *Stirred Vanilla Custard* with raspberries. In fact, this custard is so simple that it will likely become a family favorite as well.

Desserts demand a special treatment during the holidays. Extraordinary recipes are needed for parties and gift giving. *Orange Caramel Brulée* or *Pears Poached in Port Wine* are summoned for an intimate dinner party. Delightful homemade *Walnut Raisin Fudge, English Toffee,* and *Creamy Caramels* can be beautifully packaged as a gift to neighbors and friends.

Whether light or luscious, this chapter is sure to please the sweet tooth in everyone.

Pears Poached in Port Wine

4	medium pears	1	cinnamon stick
2	cups Port wine or other red wine	⅛	teaspoon ground cloves
1	cup water	1	small orange, cut into ¼-inch slices
1	tablespoon orange flavor liquer or undiluted frozen orange juice concentrate	3	tablespoons cornstarch
		⅓	cup cold water
¼	cup sugar		Whipped cream, optional
			Ground nutmeg

Peel pears; cut lengthwise into halves. Core pear halves, leaving stems intact. Combine wine, water, liqueur, sugar, cinnamon, and cloves in skillet; heat at 400° until boiling. Reduce heat to simmer, between Warm and 200°. Add pear halves, cut sides down, and orange slices; cook, covered, until pears are tender when pierced with a sharp knife, 10 to 15 minutes. Remove pears; cool to room temperature and refrigerate, covered. Strain cooking liquid; discard spices and orange slices.

Return cooking liquid to skillet; heat at 400° until boiling. Reduce heat to simmer, between Warm and 200°. Mix cornstarch and cold water in small bowl; whisk into simmering liquid. Cook until thickened, whisking constantly.

Serve pears with hot sauce poured over each serving. Garnish with whipped cream. Sprinkle lightly with nutmeg.

8 servings

Fruit and Nut Filled Apples

½	cup diced mixed dried fruit		Hot water
¼	cup finely chopped pecans	1	tablespoon cornstarch
2	tablespoons brown sugar	1	cup apple juice
2	tablespoons butter, melted		
4	large baking apples (Gala, Braeburn, or Jonagold)		

Mix fruit, pecans, brown sugar, and butter in small bowl. Reserve.

Core apples by cutting to, but not through, bottoms. Peel top one-third of each apple. Fill cavity in each apple with 2 rounded tablespoons of fruit mixture. Place filled apples in baking pan on rack in skillet. Add 1 inch of hot water to skillet. Heat at 400° until water is boiling. Reduce heat to simmer, between Warm and 200°. Cook, covered, until apples are tender, about 20 to 25 minutes.

Combine cornstarch and apple juice in small saucepan until smooth. Cook over medium heat to boiling, stirring frequently. Boil until mixture thickens and is clear, stirring constantly. Serve over warm apples.

4 servings

Stirred Vanilla Custard

4 cups half-and-half, divided	¼ cup cornstarch
⅔ cup sugar	1 tablespoon vanilla
6 eggs	1½ cups fresh sweetened raspberries

Whisk 3 cups half-and-half and sugar in skillet. Turn skillet to 350°. Heat mixture until simmering (bubbles forming around edge of pan), whisking constantly. Reduce heat to 200°.

Whisk remaining 1 cup half-and-half, eggs, cornstarch, and vanilla until well blended and smooth in medium bowl. Stir about 1 cup hot mixture into egg mixture until blended. Add egg mixture to skillet. Whisk constantly until mixture thickens, about 3 to 5 minutes. Immediately pour custard into large bowl. Continue to whisk until mixture is smooth.

Press waxed paper over surface to prevent skin from forming. Refrigerate until well chilled, about 3 to 4 hours. Serve with sweetened raspberries spooned over each serving.

8 servings

Orange Caramel Brulée

1 cup sugar, divided	1 teaspoon vanilla
2 cups half-and-half, warmed	⅛ teaspoon ground mace
3 eggs, beaten	⅛ teaspoon salt
2 tablespoons orange flavor liqueur	Warm water

Heat skillet at 300°. Add ¾ cup sugar; cook until sugar is dissolved and golden in color, stirring constantly. Turn heat to Off. Immediately pour sugar syrup into 1½-quart glass casserole. Holding casserole with pot holders, quickly tilt casserole to coat bottom and side with syrup. Let stand while preparing custard. Clean skillet.

Beat half-and-half and eggs until well blended in medium bowl; beat in remaining ¼ cup sugar, liqueur, vanilla, mace, and salt. Pour custard mixture into casserole; place casserole on rack in skillet. Add 1½ inches warm water to skillet; heat, covered, at 400° until boiling. Reduce heat to simmer, between Warm and 200°; cook, covered, until custard is set, about 30 minutes. Remove casserole from skillet; cool on wire rack to room temperature. If moisture has collected on top of custard, carefully blot with paper toweling.

Refrigerate until chilled, 3 to 4 hours. Invert custard onto rimmed serving plate.

4 servings

Rice Pudding with Raspberry Sauce

1	cup slivered almonds	⅓	cup almond flavor liqueur
3	cups milk	¼	cup butter or margarine, softened
2	cups water	2	cups whipping cream
½	cup sugar	2	tablespoons sugar
¼	teaspoon salt	1	10-ounce package frozen
⅛	teaspoon ground mace		raspberries, thawed
2	cups white long grain rice	1	tablespoon almond flavor liqueur

Heat skillet at 300°. Add almonds; heat until almonds begin to brown; stirring occasionally. Remove and reserve.

Mix milk, water, ½ cup sugar, salt, and mace in skillet; heat at 400° until boiling. Stir in rice. Reduce heat to simmer, between Warm and 200°; cook, covered, until rice is tender and liquid is absorbed, about 30 minutes, stirring occasionally. Stir in ⅓ cup liqueur and butter. Remove to large bowl; cool to room temperature.

Whip cream and 2 tablespoons sugar in bowl until stiff peaks form. Fold whipped cream into rice mixture. Fold in reserved almonds. Refrigerate, covered, until chilled, 2 to 3 hours.

Combine raspberries and 1 tablespoon liqueur in food processor or blender. Process until smooth. Refrigerate, covered, until ready to serve.

Serve rice pudding with raspberry sauce spooned over each serving.

12 servings

Cranberry Pecan Bread Pudding

2	cups milk	¼	teaspoon salt
3	tablespoons butter	4	cups ½-inch cubes dense
3	eggs, beaten		multi-grain bread
⅔	cup packed light brown sugar	1	cup dried cranberries
1	teaspoon vanilla	⅓	cup chopped pecans
½	teaspoon ground cinnamon		Hot water
¼	teaspoon ground nutmeg		

Heat milk and butter in small saucepan over medium heat until butter is melted, stirring occasionally. Combine eggs, brown sugar, vanilla, cinnamon, nutmeg, and salt in medium bowl. Stir in warm milk until combined. Stir in bread cubes, cranberries, and pecans. Spoon mixture into well-greased 2-quart casserole. Place casserole on rack in skillet. Add 1½ inches of water to skillet. Heat at 400° until water is boiling. Reduce heat to simmer, between Warm and 200°. Cook, covered, until knife inserted near center comes out clean, about 1¼ to 1½ hours. Remove casserole from skillet; cool on wire rack. Serve warm.

8 servings

Fresh Strawberry Tart

Sweet Pastry (see recipe below)
½ cup sugar
3 tablespoons all-purpose flour
⅛ teaspoon salt
1½ cups half-and-half or milk

3 egg yolks, beaten
½ teaspoon vanilla or almond extract
2 to 3 pints fresh strawberries, hulled
⅓ cup currant jelly
1 to 2 teaspoons water

Make Sweet Pastry. Invert onto serving dish; reserve.

Mix sugar, flour, and salt in skillet. Stir in half-and-half gradually until blended; cook at 200° until thickened, about 4 minutes, stirring constantly. Stir about ½ cup half-and-half mixture into egg yolks. Stir yolk mixture into skillet; cook until thickened, about 4 minutes, stirring constantly. Stir in vanilla. Remove cream mixture to bowl; cool to room temperature, stirring occasionally. Refrigerate until chilled, about 2 hours. Clean skillet.

Spread cream mixture evenly over Sweet Pastry. Arrange berries on cream, pointed ends up. Heat currant jelly and water in skillet at Warm until jelly is melted; brush jelly over strawberries.

Substitution Tip: Any fresh or drained canned fruit can be substituted for the strawberries. If using a light-colored fruit, such as pineapple, banana, or peaches, substitute apple jelly for currant jelly.

6 servings

Sweet Pastry

2 cups all-purpose flour
2 tablespoons sugar
¼ teaspoon salt

½ cup cold butter, cut into pieces
3 tablespoons vegetable shortening
5 to 6 tablespoons ice water

Mix flour, sugar, and salt in medium bowl; cut in butter and shortening until mixture resembles coarse crumbs. Mix in enough water to form smooth dough; refrigerate, covered, at least 1 hour.

Heat skillet at 300°. Roll pastry on lightly floured surface into 10-inch square; trim to 9 inches, rounding corners. Roll pastry onto rolling pin; unroll onto center of piece of aluminum foil 20 inches long. Place foil with pastry in skillet, allowing edges of foil to extend up sides of skillet. Pierce pastry with fork; cook, covered, 10 minutes, or until bottom of pastry is golden. Remove pastry from skillet by inverting it onto a wire rack. Remove aluminum foil. Place rack in skillet; increase heat to 400°, bake, covered, 15 minutes. Remove from skillet; cool on wire rack.

One 9-inch pastry

Fresh Berries in Patty Shells

½ cup sugar	1 10-ounce package frozen puff
2 tablespoons all-purpose flour	pastry shells
⅛ teaspoon salt	1½ to 2 cups fresh raspberries, blueberries,
1½ cups half-and-half or milk	or sliced strawberries
2 egg yolks, beaten	Whipped cream
½ teaspoon vanilla or almond extract	Ground nutmeg

Mix sugar, flour, and salt in skillet. Stir in half-and-half gradually until blended; cook at 200° until thickened, about 4 minutes, stirring constantly. Stir about ½ cup half-and-half mixture into egg yolks. Stir yolk mixture into skillet; cook until thickened, about 4 minutes, stirring constantly. Stir in vanilla. Remove cream mixture to bowl; cool to room temperature, stirring occasionally. Refrigerate until chilled, about 2 hours. Clean skillet.

Heat skillet at 400°. Place rack in skillet; cover with piece of parchment paper. Place frozen pastry shells on paper; cook, covered, 1 hour. Remove moist dough from centers of pastry shells with fork and discard. Continue cooking, covered, 5 minutes. Remove pastry shells from skillet; cool on wire rack.

Place pastry shells on serving plates; fill shells with berries. Spoon cream mixture over berries; garnish with whipped cream. Sprinkle lightly with nutmeg.

6 servings

Blueberry Cream Cake

1 9-ounce package yellow cake mix	1½ cups milk
1 egg	1 teaspoon orange flavor liqueur or
½ cup water	¼ teaspoon orange extract
¼ cup sour cream	1 21-ounce can blueberry pie filling
1 teaspoon grated lemon peel	1 teaspoon sugar
1 3-ounce package vanilla pudding mix	⅛ teaspoon ground cinnamon

Grease and flour 8-inch square baking pan.

Make cake mix according to package directions, using egg and water; mix in sour cream and lemon peel. Heat skillet at 350°. Pour batter into prepared pan. Place pan on rack in skillet; cook, covered, until toothpick inserted near center of cake comes out clean, about 1¼ hours. Cool cake on wire rack 5 minutes; invert onto serving plate.

Make pudding mix in skillet according to package directions, using 1½ cups milk; stir in liqueur. Remove to small bowl; cool to room temperature. Refrigerate, covered, until chilled, about 30 minutes. Spread pudding over top of cake. Mix pie filling, sugar, and cinnamon; spoon over pudding. Refrigerate until ready to serve.

9 servings

Sour Cream Rhubarb Cake

½   cup all-purpose flour
½   cup packed brown sugar
3   tablespoons butter, melted
1   teaspoon ground cinnamon
1½ cups chopped fresh rhubarb
2½ cups all-purpose flour, divided
1   teaspoon baking soda
½   teaspoon baking powder

¼   teaspoon salt
½   cup butter, softened
1¼ cups sugar
2   eggs
1½ teaspoons vanilla
⅔   cup sour cream
    Whipped cream

Mix flour, brown sugar, butter, and cinnamon in small bowl until crumbly. Reserve.

Combine rhubarb and ¼ cup flour in small bowl; mix until rhubarb is well coated with flour. Reserve.

Combine remaining 2¼ cups flour, baking soda, baking powder, and salt in small bowl. Mix butter and sugar in medium bowl; beat until light and fluffy. Beat in eggs and vanilla; add combined dry ingredients alternately with sour cream, mixing well after each addition. Gently fold in rhubarb mixture.

Preheat skillet at 275°. Pour batter evenly into skillet. Sprinkle topping mixture evenly over batter. Cook, covered, until toothpick inserted into center of cake comes out clean, about 50 to 55 minutes. Turn off skillet; uncover and let cake stand in skillet for 5 minutes. Invert cake onto cooling rack; then invert again onto second rack, so that topping side of cake is facing up. Serve warm with whipped cream, as desired.

12 servings

Peach Praline Upside-Down Cake

1¼ cups milk
1   tablespoon lemon juice
1   18¼-ounce package yellow cake mix
3   eggs
⅓   cup vegetable oil

⅓   cup butter or margarine
⅔   cup pecan halves
¾   cup packed light brown sugar
1   teaspoon maple extract
1   29-ounce can sliced peaches, drained

Mix milk and lemon juice in small bowl; let stand 15 minutes. Make cake mix according to package directions, using milk mixture, eggs, and oil. Reserve.

Heat butter in skillet at Warm until melted. Stir in pecans; cook at 200° until pecans are toasted, 3 to 5 minutes. Stir in brown sugar and maple extract; cook, until sugar is melted, stirring frequently. Arrange peach slices evenly in skillet. Spoon reserved batter over peaches; cook, with cover ½ inch ajar, at 225° until cake springs back when touched in center, 50 to 55 minutes. Invert immediately onto serving plate.

10 to 12 servings

Glazed Carrot Walnut Cake

1	9-ounce yellow cake mix	¼	teaspoon ground nutmeg
1	egg	¼	teaspoon ground ginger
½	cup water		**Browned Butter Glaze**
½	cup shredded carrots		(see recipe below)
¼	cup chopped walnuts		Walnut halves
¾	teaspoon ground cinnamon		

Grease and flour 8-inch round cake pan.

Make cake mix according to package directions, using egg and water; stir in carrots, walnuts, cinnamon, nutmeg, and ginger. Heat skillet at 350°. Pour batter into prepared pan. Place cake pan on rack in skillet; cook, with cover ½ inch ajar, until toothpick inserted near center of cake comes out clean, 40 to 45 minutes. Remove cake pan from skillet; cool on wire rack 10 minutes. Remove cake to serving plate.

Make Browned Butter Glaze; spoon glaze over cake. Garnish edge of cake with walnut halves.

6 to 8 servings

Browned Butter Glaze

¼	cup butter	1½ to 2	tablespoons milk
1	tablespoon dark corn syrup	¼	teaspoon vanilla
1	cup powdered sugar	⅛	teaspoon salt

Heat butter in skillet at Warm until melted; cook until butter is browned, about 1 minute, stirring constantly. Turn heat to Off; add corn syrup. Stir in sugar and milk alternately, using enough milk to obtain thin glaze consistency. Stir in vanilla and salt.

About ⅔ cups

Chocolate Raspberry Pudding Cake

¼	cup water		¼	cup all-purpose flour
6	ounces semi-sweet chocolate chips		⅛	teaspoon salt
2	teaspoons instant coffee crystals		1¼	cups raspberry flavor liqueur or orange juice
¾	cup butter, cut into small pieces		5	egg whites
5	egg yolks			Water
¾	cup sugar			
¼	cup cornstarch			

Grease and sugar 2-quart soufflé dish.

Heat water in skillet at Warm. Add chocolate and coffee, stirring until chocolate is melted. Stir in butter, several pieces at a time, until melted; turn heat to Off. Beat egg yolks and sugar until smooth in small bowl; stir gradually into chocolate mixture. Combine cornstarch, flour, and salt in small bowl; stir into chocolate mixture; stir in liqueur.

Beat egg whites in large bowl until stiff peaks form. Stir about a fourth of the egg whites into chocolate mixture. Fold chocolate mixture into egg whites. Clean skillet. Pour chocolate batter into prepared soufflé dish.

Place 2 or 3 metal skewers in skillet; place soufflé dish on skewers. Add 1½ inches water; heat at 400° until boiling. Reduce heat to simmer, between Warm and 200°; cook, covered, until pudding is set, about 50 minutes. Serve warm, or refrigerate until chilled and serve cold.

8 servings

Sugared Cookies

½	cup butter or margarine, softened		⅓	cup finely chopped pecans
¼	cup powdered sugar		⅛	teaspoon salt
½	teaspoon vanilla			Powdered sugar
1	cup plus 2 tablespoons all-purpose flour			

Beat butter in small bowl until fluffy; beat in sugar and vanilla. Mix in flour, pecans, and salt. Shape dough into ¾-inch balls; flatten with bottom of glass to ¼-inch thickness.

Heat skillet at 225°. Place half the cookies in bottom of skillet; cook, with cover ½ inch ajar, until golden, about 15 minutes on each side. Remove cookies to wire rack. Repeat with remaining dough. Coat warm cookies generously with powdered sugar. Cool and store in airtight container.

36 cookies

English Trifle

½ cup sugar
3 tablespoons all-purpose flour
⅛ teaspoon salt
2 cups half-and-half or milk
3 egg yolks, beaten
½ teaspoon vanilla or
  almond extract
¾ cup sliced almonds

1 10¾-ounce frozen pound cake,
  thawed
½ cup almond flavor liqueur
⅔ cup raspberry preserves
1 cup whipping cream
¼ cup powdered sugar
¼ teaspoon vanilla

Mix sugar, flour, and salt in skillet. Stir in half-and-half gradually until blended; cook at 200° until thickened, about 4 minutes, stirring constantly. Stir about ½ cup half-and-half mixture into egg yolks. Stir yolk mixture into skillet; cook until thickened, about 4 minutes, stirring constantly. Stir in vanilla. Remove cream mixture to bowl; cool to room temperature, stirring occasionally. Refrigerate until chilled, about 2 hours. Clean skillet.

Heat skillet at 300°. Add almonds; heat until almonds begin to brown, stirring occasionally. Remove and reserve.

Cut pound cake lengthwise into halves; cut into ½-inch slices. Arrange half the cake slices on bottom of straight-sided glass bowl or soufflé dish, cutting pieces, if necessary, to fill spaces. Sprinkle cake with ¼ cup liqueur; spread with ⅓ cup preserves and 1 cup cream mixture. Sprinkle with ¼ cup almonds. Repeat layers, reserving remaining ¼ cup almonds. Refrigerate, covered, 4 hours or overnight.

Whip cream until stiff peaks form, gradually adding powdered sugar and vanilla. Spread over trifle; sprinkle with reserved ¼ cup almonds.

6 to 8 servings

Chocolate-Apricot Date Bars

1 cup water	1 teaspoon vanilla
6 ounces dried apricots, finely chopped	½ cup butter or margarine
6 ounces pitted dates, finely chopped	1 18 ¼-ounce package yellow cake mix
⅓ cup sugar	1 cup quick-cooking oats
4 ounces unsweetened chocolate, coarsely chopped	1 cup chopped pecans, divided
	1 egg
	Water

Combine water, apricots, dates, and sugar in skillet; heat at 400° until boiling. Reduce heat to Warm. Stir in chocolate until melted; cook until thickened, about 8 minutes, stirring occasionally. Stir in vanilla. Remove fruit mixture and reserve. Clean skillet.

Heat butter in skillet at Warm until melted. Stir in cake mix, oats, and ½ cup pecans. Break egg into measuring cup; add enough water to make ½ cup. Stir egg mixture into skillet until well blended. Smooth batter into even layer; cook at 200°, with cover ½ inch ajar, until cake appears dry on the surface, 15 to 18 minutes. Spread reserved fruit mixture over cake. Sprinkle with remaining ½ cup pecans; cook with cover ½ inch ajar, 35 minutes. Cool in skillet before cutting.

24 bars

Fudge Brownie Ice Cream Pie

¼ cup butter or margarine	¼ cup all-purpose flour
1 ounce unsweetened chocolate, coarsely chopped	¼ teaspoon baking powder
Warm water	¼ teaspoon salt
½ cup sugar	1 quart chocolate chip or vanilla ice cream, slightly softened
1 egg, beaten	2 tablespoon sliced almonds, toasted
¼ teaspoon almond extract	Fudge ice cream topping

Grease 8-inch pie pan.

Place butter and chocolate in small metal bowl in skillet. Add 1 inch water to skillet; heat skillet at Warm until butter and chocolate are melted, stirring occasionally. Remove bowl from skillet; discard water. Beat sugar, egg, and almond extract until fluffy in medium bowl; add chocolate mixture gradually until blended. Stir in flour, baking powder, and salt until well blended. Spread batter evenly in prepared pan. Heat skillet at 350°. Place pie pan on rack in skillet; cook, covered, until brownie is firm to touch, about 30 minutes. Remove pie pan; cool on wire rack.

Spoon ice cream over brownie in pie pan; sprinkle with almonds. Freeze until hard, 8 hours or overnight. Serve with fudge topping.

8 servings

Chocolate Fudge Cheesecake

3	tablespoons butter or margarine		1	cup sugar
1	cup finely chopped pecans		¼	cup packed light brown sugar
¾	cup finely chopped walnuts		½	cup unsweetened cocoa
3	tablespoons sugar		3	eggs
½	teaspoon ground cinnamon		¼	cup whipping cream or half-and-half
2	8-ounce packages cream cheese, softened		1	teaspoon vanilla

Place butter in bottom of 9-inch springform pan. Place pan on rack in skillet; cook, covered, at 375° until butter is melted. Blend in nuts, 3 tablespoons sugar, and cinnamon; remove 2 tablespoons nut mixture and reserve. Pat remaining mixture evenly in bottom and ½ inch up side of springform pan; cook, covered, at 375° for 15 minutes.

Beat cream cheese until fluffy in large bowl. Beat in 1 cup sugar, brown sugar, and cocoa until smooth. Beat in eggs, one at a time, beating well after each addition. Mix in whipping cream and vanilla until smooth; pour into crust. Sprinkle with reserved nut mixture; cook, covered, until cheesecake is set, 40 to 45 minutes. Remove springform pan from skillet; cool to room temperature on wire rack.

Refrigerate cheesecake until chilled, 3 to 4 hours. Remove rim of springform pan before serving.

8 to 10 servings

English Toffee

1½	cups coarsely chopped almonds, divided		¼	cup water
1	cup butter		1	tablespoon light corn syrup
1⅓	cups sugar		6	ounces semi-sweet chocolate chips Warm water

Lightly grease 13 x 9 x 2-inch baking pan.

Heat skillet at 300°. Add almonds; heat until almonds begin to brown, stirring occasionally. Remove and reserve.

Heat butter in skillet at Warm until melted. Stir in sugar, water, and corn syrup; cook at 325° until candy thermometer registers 300° (hard crack), stirring constantly. Turn heat to Off. Stir in 1 cup reserved almonds. Pour toffee mixture into prepared pan; cool to room temperature.

Place chocolate in small metal bowl in skillet. Add 1 inch water to skillet; heat skillet at Warm until chocolate is melted, stirring occasionally. Spread chocolate evenly over toffee; sprinkle with remaining ½ cup almonds. Refrigerate until chocolate is hard, about 15 minutes. Break candy into pieces with tip of knife. Store in airtight container.

About 1¼ pounds

Chocolate Clusters

1	pound semi-sweet chocolate, coarsely chopped		Warm water
2	ounces unsweetened chocolate, coarsely chopped	2	cups cocktail peanuts
		1½	cups raisins

Place chocolate in metal bowl in skillet. Add 1½ inches water to skillet. Heat skillet at Warm until chocolate is melted, stirring occasionally. Stir in peanuts and raisins; remove bowl from skillet.

Drop chocolate mixture by rounded tablespoonfuls onto waxed paper-lined cookie sheet. Refrigerate until hard, about 15 minutes. Store candies in airtight container.

About 1¾ pounds

Chocolate Almond Bark

2½	cups blanched whole almonds	2	ounces unsweetened chocolate, coarsely chopped
1	pound semi-sweet chocolate, coarsely chopped		Warm water

Heat skillet at 300°. Add almonds; heat until almonds begin to brown, stirring occasionally. Remove and reserve.

Place chocolate in metal bowl in skillet. Add 1½ inches water to skillet. Heat skillet at Warm until chocolate is melted, stirring occasionally. Stir in reserved almonds; remove bowl from skillet.

Spread mixture to ¼-inch thickness on waxed paper-lined cookie sheet. Refrigerate until hard, about 15 minutes; break into pieces. Store candies in airtight container.

About 2 pounds

Walnut Raisin Fudge

1	pound semi-sweet chocolate, coarsely chopped	1½	teaspoons vanilla
1	14-ounce can sweetened condensed milk	⅛	teaspoon salt
		¾	cup chopped walnuts
		½	cup raisins

Combine chocolate, condensed milk, vanilla, and salt in skillet. Heat skillet at Warm until chocolate is melted, stirring frequently. Stir in walnuts and raisins. Pour into aluminum foil-lined 8 x 8-inch baking pan. Refrigerate until firm, about 15 minutes. Cut into squares. Store in airtight container.

1½ pounds

Mixed Nut Brittle

2	cups mixed nuts	½	cup water
1	cup sugar	¼	cup butter
1	cup packed light brown sugar	1½	teaspoons baking soda
1	cup light corn syrup		

Grease jelly roll pan.

Heat skillet at 300°. Add nuts; heat until nuts begin to brown, stirring occasionally. Remove and reserve. Clean skillet.

Mix sugars, corn syrup, and water in skillet; cook at Warm until sugars dissolve, stirring occasionally. Continue cooking at 300° until mixture boils. Stir in butter until melted; continue cooking until candy thermometer registers 300° (hard crack). Turn heat to Off. Stir in reserved nuts and soda; pour mixture into prepared pan, spreading quickly with spatula. Cool to room temperature. Break into pieces. Store in airtight container.

About 2 pounds

Creamy Caramels

2	cups whipping cream or half-and-half, divided	1	cup packed light brown sugar
¾	cup light corn syrup	½	cup butter
1	cup sugar	¾	cup chopped pecans

Combine 1 cup cream, corn syrup, sugars, and butter in skillet; cook at Warm until butter is melted, stirring occasionally. Stir in remaining 1 cup cream; cook at 300° until boiling. Continue cooking until candy thermometer registers 245° (firm ball), stirring constantly. Turn heat to Off; stir in pecans. Pour candy into aluminum foil-lined 8 x 8-inch baking pan. Cool; cut into squares. Wrap individually in waxed paper; twist ends.

60 caramels

Recipe Index